A Parent's Guide to Teen Social Media

What Your Kids Aren't Telling You

Bjorn Beam

A Parent's Guide to Teen Social Media:

What Your Kids Aren't Telling You

ISBN: 979-8-6426757-5-5 *(Paperback)*

First printing edition 2020.

www.SecuritySquad.org

Table of Contents

Introduction

You are responsible for everything you post, and everything you post will be a reflection of you.

—Germany Kent, Social Media Etiquette Expert[1]

If someone had told you thirty years ago that you would be competing for your child's attention with a tiny little electronic box, you probably would have laughed.[i] However, that perfectly articulates the problem we are facing with social media today—it's something so new, so fast-paced, and so invasive that we do not know what to do with it. We don't know what to make of it. And most importantly, we don't know how to shield our children from the dangers that loom within the digital walls of each social media app. But before we walk down the halls of social media, we need to first step back and talk about the internet.

With the rise of the internet, all of a sudden, you can share intimate information, knowledge, and photos and have them blasted to the entire world. The internet is infinite—its limitless potential is not something we have had time to digest. In the past, anything, whether it was earning potential or the number of letters you could send out every year, had a cap. Being limitless was not possible,

---

[i] In 1976, Mattel introduced the first handheld electric gaming system, but it was not until 1989 that Nintendo dominated the market with the release of the Game Boy.

simply because we did not have the technology for being limitless. And we probably liked it that way, because, at the end of the day, our brains can't understand limitlessness, infinity, or eternity.[2]

It's true; there is actual scientific proof that our brains are not able to understand the concept of forever. That's why we are so uncomfortable with topics of death, the afterlife, higher powers, or just forever and eternity—we can't actually understand what they mean. How are we able to comprehend limitlessness when we cannot comprehend $23 trillion, the current and growing US national debt?

I am not saying all of this to make this book sound like some spiritual journey guide or make us feel little in the face of the power of what infinity means. It's just that we have to acknowledge the vast scale of social media to approach the problem. Social media has thrust this kind of infinite eternity right in our face. And it scares us. It scares the government. They are trying feverishly to exert some kind of control over the monopolistic social media companies that are influencing how you and I talk, think, and buy today. As companies that exist in the private sector, these apps are able to make policies that really should be regulated by a government because they can impact the entire world.

But as it stands today, there is no regulatory agency, no special laws, and no third-party brand of oversight that mandates what can and cannot happen on these social media apps. It's the Wild, Wild West, and your children are out playing in it. In fact, they're out on their horses, guns in holster, roaming around towns and saloons, discovering gold mines and other resources that have never been discovered until now. All I ever discovered were some tires lodged in the creek behind our house, and a smashed soup can, waiting to give me tetanus every time I touched it.

Yet the same gift of the expanse of the internet has some negative aspects, as a lot of bad things have also happened because of it. The fact remains that there are many people out there who wish they never got on the internet. If it isn't the plundered finances of some, it is the little kid who lost his/her life to suicide because of cyberbullying. To such people, the internet is a curse, one that could have been avoided at one point or another.

How can one thing be a gift and yet a curse at the same time? The answer is, it depends on how it is used. The internet thrives on information exchange. Information exchange is built on the data that internet users either upload or download. So, in essence, the internet can be regarded as a storehouse or a bottomless well of information and data that anyone can draw from, provided they know how to get the information. This principle makes the internet a dangerous place to be when you do not take the right precautions. This is because the internet has become a watering hole for cybercriminals and questionable data companies, all of whom are thirsty for confidential data and information that they can apply to nefarious ends. However, while we can throw up our hands and say we are done interacting with the internet, it is constantly interacting with us. Back in the day, the sound of a dialup modem would let us know we were connected to the digital world. Now our laptops, cellphones, smartwatches, and Internet of Things (IoT) devices, like our TVs, are constantly communicating with the outside world.

If you are like most people, you probably hate the feeling of having this lawless control you cannot limit. As a parent, you want to be able to protect your children from everyone and everything—at all times. There is nothing worse than feeling hopeless in the face of a threat. The threats that loom in social media aren't normal threats either—they are not robbers outside, ready to break down the house door. They are mental threats, suicidal threats, sexual threats, and coercion threats that can steal your child away from you invisibly. On top of this, there is usually no physical trail or indication that this threat ever existed. But the victim's life is spread across the metaphorical crime scene floor for all to see.

You likely know all of this already, which is why you are reading this book today. I applaud you for taking the first step toward understanding this new world of technology that is not going anywhere anytime soon. We are staring down the sixteen-year anniversary of Facebook, which changed our world forever when it launched in February 2004.[3] Since Facebook, dozens of social media sites have entered the scene—and managed to solidify a foothold that is respectable enough to give Facebook a run for their money.

Just to give you a snapshot of the larger social media landscape today, here are the top eight most used platforms:[4]

- *Facebook: 2.23 billion users*
- *YouTube: 1.9 billion*
- *Instagram: 1 billion*
- *Qzone: 563 million*
- *Weibo: 376 million*
- *Reddit: 330 million*
- *Pinterest: 200 million*
- *Twitter: 126 million*

"But, Mom, I Want to Fit In."

In the coming chapter, we are going to delve deeper into social media statistics and make an argument for why it's here to stay. We start off the book by getting everything out on the table so social media skeptics realize the conversation needs to change from "when it goes away" to "how my family can live amicably in a world with social media." If you already have accepted that social media is here to stay, great! Skim Chapter 1 and roll up your sleeves for Chapter 2.

As you can see above, anyone who's anyone is on social media. No, it doesn't encapsulate the entire world, but it encapsulates just about every person working and living in a Western society or the digitally connected world. If you live in the United States, Canada, the UK, the EU, or anywhere else with available Wi-Fi and smart devices that won't break the bank, then you are surrounded by social media users. Even if you do not have your own account, there is likely data on you out there. This can be from a photo at a friend's birthday party or a work event, both of which were published on either an individual or a company's social media page. And there you are tagged in it, not even knowing. It is always good to google yourself and your kids' names every now and then to see what images or posts are being publicly displayed about you and them.

That's why you can't stop your teens from getting on social media. Forcing them to have no profiles may make them bigger victims of bullying at school. Your teens want to fit in, and they have the right to fit in. Withholding social media from them is going to make it taboo and only fuel their desire to learn more about what you are hiding from them. Cutting out social media cold turkey isn't the answer—but you know this.

Your teen wants to fit in, and you want them to fit in, too. Therefore, you need to learn how to coexist in the world with social media. As I am going to say over and over again in this book, social media is not going anywhere. You might want it to—it ruins your days, you do not understand it, and you just wish everything could go back to the way it was when you were growing up. As humans, we do not enjoy change, so that is a normal reaction. We get it.

Change is never easy, but it is inevitable. Our entire world is dictated by change. So much change happens every day that entire hour-long news segments can be crafted every single night, simply highlighting what happened in a single day. Change is what pushes civilization toward the future—for better or for worse. I think we can all agree that this statement sums up social media perfectly: it has brought amazing and terrible changes to the world. That's why we all have a love-hate relationship with it.

Check Your Social Media Phobia at the Door

Depending on your age, you may have a certain amount of social media phobia. However, it is hard to monitor your teen's social media usage if you do not first understand it. We do not like to feel dumb or out of the loop, which is why many parents avoid learning about social media altogether. It is a universe that your kids know more about than you—which can make you feel stupid and at the mercy of your teen. It is a weird role reversal none of us ever wants to deal with.

That is why I am asking you to check your social media phobia at the door. Part of this *Parent's Guide to Teen Social Media* is that you first understand what social media is, how you can monitor it more effectively, and how you can know what your teens are actually doing when they sign onto social media. Your teen knows what you do not know, and they use that to their advantage. Knowledge is power, and with the right knowledge, you don't have to feel like an outsider anymore. It is just essential that you release all preconceived notions, allowing this guide to equip you with the information you've been lacking. Most importantly, make your learning fun. Maybe you'll find out that you can apply some of these digital lessons learned in your workplace. I would call that a win-win.

You Want the Best for Your Teens

I'm going to level the playing field as we get started here. You want the very best for your kid. We all do. We would do anything for them. We would kill, die, and sacrifice anything in an instant. If you sat down with your husband, wife, or partner right now, you would both agree you want the following for your teen(s):

- **Happiness:** At the end of the day, every parent wants their child to be happy. They want a life of happiness for their child. One in which they smile, laugh, and love every day, from the moment they wake up to the moment they fall asleep.

    Healthiness: We want our kids to be healthy. We want them to be vigorous and energetic and full of vibrancy. Healthiness is conducive to success, happiness, and everything else you want for your teen in this life.

- **Simplicity:** Life is easiest when it's simple. None of us want complexity. You want things to be easy, simple, and amicable for your teens.

It's time to ensure that kind of life for your teen—*even* in an age of social media. I believe all of these things can coexist. It just will take some time, patience, and education.

The Age of Technology

Technology has infiltrated everything we do, from checking the temperature outside while sitting in bed, to freelancing for your income right at home. Technology books your flights, alerts you about road closures, and helps you prep dinners more quickly. Technology is the very fabric of our lives, and your kids have grown up in a world of technology. To them, it's normal. It's not bad—so why are you treating it so terribly?

A new perspective not only will make you more apt at understanding social media, but it will also win over your child's respect. When they realize that you are "hip" to the world of technology, they won't see your ideas and suggestions as attacks on their way of life. They will see the constructive criticism for what it really is and what it's really meant to be.

That's all you want, and that's all I want for you, too. Families are at stake, lives are being threatened, suicide is becoming more common, and alienation is tearing our society apart. We need to all do something about it.

It starts with the social media universe that your teens immerse themselves in every single second they are home after school. And when I say the word *universe*, I don't mean it lightly. There are subcultures, secret apps, the dark web, meme languages, emojis, cryptocurrencies, and a variety of other tech-related communication tools and norms that define this new kind of social immersion. If you think downloading app blockers or parental monitoring apps secretly on your children's phones will work, you are wrong. There are other apps designed to disable these apps, rendering them defunct. And when this happens, you not only find yourself having paid for an ineffective product, but now you're also laden with resentment and suspicion from your children. In trying to understand and control your child's digital life, do not drive a wedge between you and them, and make them take their activities underground.

Finally, in this digital globalization age, we have to come to terms with the fact that the internet provides a safe way for us to operate. I'm writing this book as I sit here in Spain during the COVID-19 coronavirus outbreak lockdown. Those that can communicate and work in a digital environment will thrive, as they can conduct their work anywhere with a computer and cellphone. According to global health experts, viruses like COVID-19 will become increasingly common in our interconnected world, coinciding with globalization, urbanization, and climate change.[5]

The fact is, the internet and social media are here to stay, so you have to work with your child to use them wisely, not alienate them or keep them from using these tools.

Data Privacy

The purpose of talking about keeping your child safe when using social media is to protect them. To protect them emotionally from the weird things online that are disturbing, to protect them from cyberbullies and predators (discussed in my previous book *Cyberbullying Crash Course: Protect Your Kids from Cyberbullies, Cyber Violence, and Digital Peer Pressure*), and to protect their overall future. I will touch on all of these but focus on the final piece: their future. This is a nebulous term, but when you consider the extent to which the internet has a hold on your child's life, you have to question how all of the data being produced by your child and about your child will impact their future. Data is not going away, and this means what is put out on the internet about them can come back to haunt their future social, career, and college opportunities, not to mention future loans. In this digital world, sadly, we are what our data says we are, and that will only increasingly haunt us as artificial intelligence (AI) systems begin to quickly process and manage this data. Any social media post or message that gets captured online could be archived, analyzed, and processed to determine the outcome of your child's financial or academic application. For example, the AI system could determine your child has anger issues based on the overuse of capital letters, exclamation points, and certain phrases in their tweets and social media posts.

So are you ready to tackle the elephant in the room head-on? Let's do this.

Chapter 1

Social Media Is Here to Stay

Give everyone the power to share anything with anyone. [6]
—Mark Zuckerberg

About fifteen years ago, the entire world changed forever when four Harvard students decided to create a platform where students could share statuses and photos. The students originally intended it to be just for Harvard, as well as other Ivy League Schools.[7] They figured it would be an easy way for people to stay up-to-date, post about parties, and do everything else that Myspace tried to achieve a few years prior.

As you can imagine, things got rocky for the four students when Facebook blew up. Who owned Facebook? Who would be the CEO? Was there room for everyone on this ride to absolute stardom? Plenty of drama and fighting went down, but we all know who emerged victorious: Mark Zuckerberg. He solidified his title as the creator of the modern world of social media, the one that defines your life, my life, and the future of our society right now. That's a lot of power for just one person.

Once Facebook made its way out of the Ivy League circle in 2004, its permanence was guaranteed. Why? Because Facebook was able to do something no other app, website, or person had been able to

11

do before in history: it was able to connect us forever. As a social network grows in size, so does the magnetic attraction to join this network over others. This network effect only strengthens the value of the network and the data within that network, which is controlled by one company, Facebook.

A taste of this kind of togetherness became a drug—people couldn't get enough. Thousands of people around the world began to create Facebook accounts. "Have you heard about this new website that enables you to share information with your followers?" High school students joined, and then young professionals, and finally, parents your age. Facebook saturated the world and made a global marketplace the likes of which the world had never seen before.

Suddenly, Zuckerberg was tasked with the responsibility of safety and protection for billions of users that spanned the entire globe. Facebook was not necessarily prepared for this kind of saturation. This is why there were plenty of transgressions along the way, like selling consumer data to companies for a profit,[8] meddling in elections,[9] and accidentally leaving up disturbing content, like people being shot in the head or individuals jumping off of buildings to their deaths. How do you police a market that big, all of the time?

That's why plenty of other social media companies popped up around the same time. Two years after Facebook's launch came Twitter, the zany one-liner social media site designed to be just about captions, texts, and comebacks. Almost six years later, Instagram came onto the scene, proposing the idea of just sharing photos/videos with no captions, updates, or statuses. Facebook keenly acquired the app, which is presently the fastest-growing social media app in the world. One year after Instagram came

Snapchat, introducing fleeting content that "disappeared" after the image was opened.

Twitter tried their hand at videos with Vine, which has since been canceled. There were blog sites like Tumblr, which threatens to close today following its ban on porn that led to a staggering thirty percent drop in users.[10] In 2016, TikTok launched, taking the idea of Vine (video editing) and bringing it one step further. It paid off, as TikTok is one of the most popular social media apps among young users—especially your teen—today. However, its use for nefarious purposes is quite concerning, which will be discussed later.

Social media is ever-changing, which is what makes it so overwhelming to understand. Facebook is lagging in sign-ups, but it's WhatsApp messaging app is soaring with downloads worldwide. Remember, Facebook also has Instagram to help boost use by the younger generation that is interested in picture exchanges. Twitter is struggling, but YouTube continues to be the second-largest search engine after Google, its parent company. It's hard to keep up but essential to understand the background story so that all of it makes sense. However, one thing is constant: significant data brokers are in this sandbox playing Whack-a-Mole as they look for the next big thing to hold the attention of their userbase and their ability to market the power of their network. The Facebooks and Googles of the world will fight to hold onto the data they have collected in their effort to grow their empires.

Social Media Is Here to Stay

Why is social media here to stay? Why am I so confident this new way of communication isn't going anywhere? Here are the top six reasons why social media will only grow in prominence and importance:

1. **It Connects Us:** Biologically, we are wired to connect.[11] Humans have evolved to require community, communication, and connection to survive. It's why we can talk and say words. Our brains need connection and collaboration with other humans. Isolation is not something natural or healthy for our souls. We are our happiest when surrounded by people we love, who love us in return.

   Therefore, social media feeds one of the most innate human desires. It enables you to stay connected with those you love the most. You can see where they are, what they are doing, what they are feeling, and how they are looking. You can feel a connection that is almost like being in the same room with them. Although it's not quite the same thing, why would we ever turn our backs on something that permits us to watch our kids every single day? It's the same as someone asking you if you'd want one of your deceased loved ones brought back for a day. The answer is: of course! Most amazingly, no human is immune to this desire! Not you, nor I, nor the President of the United States. It's a great equalizer that we all must submit to. I bet it's even safe to say that you have checked your social media today, right?

2. **It Gives Us Attention:** Who doesn't want some attention? No matter our age, where we live, or what we look like, we all crave that "pat on the back" every now and then. Of course, some of us crave it a little more than others. Regardless, social media provides us with attention and self-validation. When you post a picture of your breakfast on social media and make a joke about it, the likes and comments on the post make you feel seen, funny, and important.

That kind of attention is infectious. It's the same biological driving force that makes us all yearn to be "popular" in high school. We care what others think about us. In fact, we care immensely.[12] It can be this singular human experience that makes so many people addicted to social media.

And just for a moment, think about this factor for your teen. When we are in our teenage years, we feel awkward, uncomfortable in our bodies, and desperate for validation that we are hot or desirable. Posting pictures on social media, whether edited or altered, is a way for teens to get that validation they might not be getting in the classroom.

For teens that don't post pictures, they're seen as "weird," simply because everyone else is doing it. Groupthink can be a dangerous human condition, and it's one that has certainly wreaked havoc on our history in the past. To their peers, those who don't post become outsiders, anomalies for not taking part in this ritual of digital interaction.

3. **It Enables Us to Snoop:** Be honest—in the last month, you've signed on to social media to stalk someone. I don't mean stalk in a dangerous sense; I mean, you have gone through their profile, read all of their comments, and looked at all of their most recent photos. Perhaps you took it a step further and went through their personal information, cross-checking it on all of their social profiles. Or maybe, just maybe you typed their name into a Google search. That's not social media, right? However, when you typed their name into Google and saw a picture of them at some event, did you notice if that was visible because they or someone they are connected to did not have high privacy settings on their social media account? It's interesting how social media is everywhere.

Regardless of the extent, social media feeds our desire to snoop. Humans have been snooping since the beginning of time, exploring theories, thoughts, and misconceptions about bosses, neighbors, and friends. Maybe you want to snoop because someone used to be your best friend and no longer is, or you want to check up on an ex-boyfriend/ex-girlfriend.

You might want to snoop before a blind date. You also might want to snoop before you say yes to a prospective roommate you barely know. There are many times when snooping comes in handy. There are also times when purely negative feelings fuel snooping. You might want to snoop to feel better about yourself or spread gossip. You might want to snoop to break up a relationship. You might want to snoop to make up lies.

No matter where your desire to spy comes from, social media makes it way too easy to feed it. That's not exactly something any of us want to pass up. You just need to remember, if you are doing it, others are definitely looking up your name too. Stalk yourself a bit and Google your name. You may be surprised at what is out there that you didn't know about.

4. **It Grows Our Businesses:** Let us think about social media from a business standpoint for a moment. Social media represents the biggest block of users in the entire world. Running an ad on Facebook gives you the potential to reach billions of people (if the right funds are allocated). With the filters and targeting capabilities on social sites today, you can reach niche consumers more efficiently than ever before. You can tell the social sites that you want to sell to women in their forties with brown hair and blue eyes. You

can tell Facebook that you want to retarget users that have already shopped for sofas. Or maybe women in their forties with kids between the ages of twelve and fifteen that have already looked for sofas.

The sky is the limit. You can also engage in inbound marketing by posting great content, blogs, images, and videos on your business profiles every day. With this kind of enticing content, you can persuade people to visit your business platform, piquing their interest in your business and what they stand to gain from investing in you. This interest may be a book about your teens and social media, but this should speak to your own business interests.

At a teen level, there is also the world of influencing. Known as *influencer marketing*, teens can grow their social accounts if they have a specific niche or engaging concept, and actually make money from YouTube videos, promotions, etc. In fact, influencer marketing is on track to be worth $15 billion by 2022.[13] If you dismissed this kind of marketing in the past, I challenge you to think again. However, the critical part here is your kids are using various social media platforms that can run highly targeted advertising and influencing campaigns. Some sites may be better than others in limiting marketing, but a user on a free platform is just that, a target for marketing or selling data. I will go into the selling of data later.

5. **It Feeds Our Imaginations:** As adults, it can feel like we lack in the wanderlust and imagination that once captivated our minds and hearts. Letting go of those fantasies, like Mickey Mouse or Barney the Dinosaur, is a part of growing up. However, it doesn't mean that as an adult, you are entirely without any imagination at all.

We still have dreams, desires, and passions that we long to feed. Maybe you wish you could travel more; perhaps you want to watch celebrities get on and off of their yachts; maybe you want to learn a new craft that you never dared to learn in your younger years. Social media is a treasure trove of information and imagery that can feed your dreams and imagination. You no longer need to wonder what Croatia looks like from a sailboat—you can literally watch someone sail around its coasts, right through Instagram.

Dreaming helps us make it through our mundane days and lives. Same with your teens. It's hard to look away from the gorgeously curated content that makes us feel like we are finally at peace with our pleasures and passions.

6. **It Helps Us Procrastinate:** We all procrastinate. Psychology states that we procrastinate because we are afraid of failing the tasks at hand. Instead of failing, we would rather not do them at all, coasting through life without upsetting anyone, including ourselves. Procrastination is a natural psychological state, one that you and I have probably engaged in already today.

That brings me to the final point of social media and why we love it: social media makes it easy to avoid doing the things you should be doing. It's a lot easier to watch your aunt and cousin fight in the comment section of a Facebook picture than it is to read a book, write a paper, or complete a work project. When we don't want to do something, we open up Instagram and start wasting our time. It's also a second-nature habit for when we are bored. It's much easier just to click an app than it is to start a puzzle or go outside and do landscaping work. None of us are immune.

With that, I will conclude my argument for why social media is here to stay.

What Is the Official Definition of Social Media?

Social media can be accessed via computers, laptops, tablets, and, most importantly, phones. In fact, nearly eighty percent of social media usage time is spent on mobile devices.[14] Basically, social media is just a tap away for your teen at all times. Even if you take it off of their phones, they'll use it on their friends' phones, on school computers, or at afterschool facilities. They can even access it at a library. That's how prominent it is and why you shouldn't approach the social media problem from a flat "ban" point of view.

How Many Social Media Apps Does Your Teen Use?

On average, your teen in the bracket of fifteen to eighteen will use four social media apps regularly, while younger teens of thirteen to fifteen will use three social media apps.[15] That means just cracking down on Facebook or Instagram won't curb their entire social media usage. It also means an elementary understanding of Facebook and maybe Instagram won't help you understand what's happening on Snapchat and TikTok. Furthermore, for your kids, each of these apps has a unique purpose to them. Facebook is for family, Instagram for friends, Snapchat for friends and boyfriends/girlfriends, and TikTok for self-expression. This, of course, is a simplification. In reality, the landscape is a mix of a mosaic and a Venn diagram. This is particularly true with the use of the various chat features in these different sites.

Later in this book, I'm going to go over some social media app nuances that will help you understand these lesser-known apps more thoroughly, so you don't have to feel like such an outsider.

At this point, you understand that social media is here, it's powerful, and it's influential over your teen and us all. You know that your teen most definitely will use it, even if you ban it. You know that they will use multiple social media apps at once, dispersing their usage over different social universes that you might not know.

That brings us to the first "fun" chapter of this book: What are teens actually doing online? It's probably the golden question you ask yourself every single day. Let's explore it further.

Chapter 2

What Are Teens Actually Doing Online?

Social media is addictive precisely because it gives us something which the real world lacks: it gives us immediacy, direction, and value as an individual.[16]
—David Amerland

When your child comes home from school, gets off the school bus, and rushes into the house, they probably have their head buried in their smartphone, tablet, or smartwatch. You try to ask them how their day was, only to get a shrug, a grimace, or no answer at all. School is hard when you are a teenager; we have all been there.

As you try to make conversation to the best of your ability, your teen slips away from your grasp, right into the digital world in the palm of their hand. The more you talk, the less they listen, tapping away, with their thumbs going a mile a minute. You probably wonder and think to yourself: "What is my child actually doing online?"

It's a fair question to ask because, at the end of the day, not many parents know. Kids are engaging in their own language, group chats, and direct messages that are much less public than their Facebook profiles. It is in these secret avenues that the most damage can be done, which is why it's vital to learn more about what your teen is actually doing online. It's time to unpack!

Lying About Their Age

Many social media sites, like Facebook, will have an age limit to try to prevent someone as young as eleven from using their platform. However, teens know how to change the year requirement and make a Facebook profile at an age that is technically too young to be using it. So if you think that your teen is going to obey these age limits and stay away from sites that deem them "too young," think again.

That's why, according to a report released by Influence Central, the average kid gets their first smartphone at 10.3, which means they open their first social media account by 11.4. By the time they're twelve, at least fifty percent of kids will be using one social media platform, lying about their age to make it happen.[17]

When one signs up for Facebook, the sign-up process asks the user to state their age, including the year. It is way too easy for anyone to lie about their age and tell Facebook they are fifteen, when in reality, they are twelve. To some of these kids, this is a sign of rebellion, but in fact, it is them just trying to fit in with their friends. This is an issue for every site since there are regulations on how private data should be handled for minors. This goes beyond them violating a sign-up policy to exposing their identity and life to a barrage of marketing campaigns and companies grabbing their data for marketing. Chapter 5 covers these privacy issues in greater detail.

Adding Friends They Do Not Know

A big concern on these social media sites is that kids are trying to grow their networks as a popularity competition without understanding the need to limit the friends they accept. On all social media sites, users can receive "friend requests" from people they don't know. This process is different on different apps, which is why we'll provide a brief rundown now:

- **Facebook:** Even if a profile is "public" for viewing, users must send a friend request to become "friends" with a person. The user can elect to accept or decline the request, as well as delete the user at any time if they do not want to be friends with them anymore.

- **Twitter:** If a Twitter account is private, then a user must request to follow the person to view their tweets. If the Twitter account is public, the user does not need to follow the person to see their tweets.

- **Instagram:** If the Instagram account is private, a user must request to follow the person to view their posts. Depending upon how privatized the account is, the user may still be able to view their Instagram Stories, which are similar to Snapchat's (informal looped content that disappears after twenty-four hours). If the Instagram account is public, anyone can interact with the posts.

- **Snapchat:** Snapchat has a process similar to Instagram's. Additionally, Snapchat has a worrisome feature whereby individuals can see someone's location *if they have the "map" feature turned on*. Make sure you talk to your teen about this.

All other social media sites follow a similar setup. Therefore, your child should have all of their profiles set to private and the highest level of private. You should also talk with them about accepting friend requests from people they don't know. We will discuss this in greater detail later, but remember, setting your profile to private does not mean that it is "truly" private. Teach your child the *Washington Post* test, or a version of it. If your child would not want the whole world, including their parents and grandparents, to see whatever they are posting, then they should not post it.

When asked if they accept friend requests from strangers, the majority of teens say yes. Why? It increases their "follower count," which is one of the most essential metrics when gauging someone's popularity and "hotness." Many teens also allow strangers to view their content so they can appear more popular.

As you can imagine, sometimes these strangers are sex offenders or pedophiles trying to view content that should be private. Even if they are not the worst of the worst, these strangers may still not be who they say they are. They can pose as friends or interested lovers to gain the attention of the teens, as well as make fake accounts and "catfish" the teen (pretending to be someone else to gain the attention of an internet user). Regardless of the catfishing issue, why should your child be sharing the most intimate parts of their life?

According to the Pew Research Center, one in six teens (seventeen percent) and thirty-one percent of social networking teens have "friends" on their social media sites that they have never personally met. (This statistic is nearly ten years old, and sporadic data shows that the numbers have only increased since then.)[18] Unfortunately, this can be due to teens' altered sense of reality and danger, having never experienced anything catastrophic in their lives. They can't fully grasp the issue of adding someone they do not know, giving them access to their personal and sensitive information.

Chat Privately with Friends and Potential Partners

Every single social media site today comes with a private messaging tool. These companies are in competition with one another, which means when Facebook introduced Facebook Messenger, the other apps had to follow suit. These avenues make it easy to keep users within the apps, without requiring public postings and comments that can give a lot of teens anxiety today.

With Instagram and Twitter, direct messaging can occur between individual users, as well as within groups that contain two or more people. Facebook has an entire messaging service called Messenger, LinkedIn has its inbox feature, TikTok has direct messaging, and the list goes on.

Here is where your teen is thriving. Within these boxes, they can write to their friends and boyfriends/girlfriends all night long. These messages are not like texting, so you won't necessarily see the texts popping up on their phones. Instead, they are embedded in their social media apps, making them hard to locate, monitor, and find.

When a teen is messaging in a private social media thread, they are probably doing the following:

- **Bonding with Their Friends:** This is the most harmless and most used messaging purpose. Teens want to talk with their friends—you can remember! Direct messaging is where they can keep up with their friends and share images, gifs, videos, and memes. It has become the new playground, enabling everyone to stay connected and bonded, sharing laughs, hardships, and pertinent information that brings friends closer together. There's nothing wrong with this kind of social media usage, which can help your teen feel seen and supported.

- **Cyberbullying:** Unfortunately, a lot of cyberbullying and cyberhate happen in our world today. About one in five teenagers, according to Digital Trends, will be a victim of cyberbullying.[19] Many teens will engage in the act of bullying online and not even realize it. That's because it's so easy to slander other students and mock them online today—simply sending one picture around a thread of everyone at the school will totally humiliate a student. Next thing you know, your teen has helped bully a student at school that is now depressed, hospitalized, or even worse, considering suicide.

  It's entirely possible for your teen to be a victim as well. There are telling signs if they are victims of cyberbullying, which we will cover later in this book. If you suspect your teen is being cyberbullied, then it's definitely time for you, the parent, to step in and do something about it. (See Cyberbullying Crash Course: Protect Your Kids from Cyberbullies, Cyber Violence, and Digital Peer Pressure for a detailed analysis of cyberbullying.)

- **Gossiping:** Gossip is a natural part of the human condition. We can't help but get together and talk about someone else, what they were wearing, what they said, or what they did at school. Although it's not an admirable part of human nature, it is natural, which is why your teen is going to have situations where they chat with their friends about other kids in school. This can be relatively harmless unless the gossiping goes into the realm of cyberbullying. This is when

the pieces of gossip are made public, now taking the chatter
to the victim. It is important to talk to your teen about
keeping all gossip private (which means being aware that
the people they are messaging could take a screenshot and
share it with everyone).

- **Flirting:** Again, we all flirt. During our teen years, we start to
  develop feelings for others and figure out how we can make
  our attraction known. Our teen years are our most awkward
  romantic years, which is what makes phones so attractive.
  It's much easier to send text messages and images to a
  crush as opposed to talking to them in person. Therefore, a
  lot of flirting is happening online—it's where relationships
  are founded today.

  There is nothing wrong with a teen developing feelings for
  someone and expressing their adoration. There is
  something very wrong with sharing nude photos or other
  imagery that could ruin a teen's reputation for life. Be sure
  to explain this difference to your teen, underscoring the
  permanence of information and images sent through social
  media today.

- **Unknowingly Interacting with a Predator:** Although social
  media is not littered with online predators, they are still at
  large, and your teen should be aware. Predators know social
  media is the perfect place to find teens today. (They even
  know their favorite apps, which we will cover below.) They
  go onto these apps and send follow requests. They even
  take their time to buddy up to your teen, winning over their
  trust so that they wield just as much control over your kid as
  you do. The people doing this aren't necessarily fifty-year-
  old men either. They could just as likely be the high school
  senior down the road. We need to break down the

traditional image of a predator and understand it is anyone looking to take advantage of your child.

Students can even engage in catfishing just because they have a crush on someone and know they are "way out of their league." Spending months, if not years, investing in someone who isn't even real can really take a toll on your kid's mental health and trust. ***Therefore, one of the biggest concerns of yours as a parent with a teen on social media should be catfishing.***

Being aware of this kind of communication and bonding occurring through social media apps will put you in more of a protective position over your teen. You can't stop your teen from using these direct messaging features, but you can make them aware of the dangers, as well as share with them your intimate knowledge so they know they can come to you if they need help or support.

Gen Z's Favorite Social Media Apps

As we have mentioned already, younger teens today don't want to be on the same social media apps as their parents. Facebook has been swallowed by baby boomers, which is why the average teen won't use Facebook or share information on it today. The smart ones may curate a responsible image on Facebook to show future colleges and employers, working it as a decoy from the apps they are using.

If you think checking Facebook will give you the total scope of your teen's social media usage, think again. They are eons ahead of you with what apps they are using, reserving their expression for online communities that have virtually zero adults using them today.

Before diving into the leading social media apps for kids, I want to highlight some very real concerns that may come from social media. I already mentioned cyberbullying, which is a big one, but there is also the toxic mirror of self-worth that occurs. This is not anything new with the rise of social media, but we see the problem intensify with the current generations who grew up in the social media world. Research has linked social media use to body image concerns, body surveillance, dieting issues, self-objectification, and much more.[20, 21] Another study showed that female college students using Facebook were more likely to consider their self-worth by their looks than any other quality.[22] This is just the tip of the iceberg. Seeing airbrushed, wealthy, beautiful people wears down teens' self-esteem. Therefore, it is essential to keep this overarching concern in mind when observing how the various mediums of social media apps interact with your child's self-perception.

Although there is an entire market of dark social media apps that your teens will try, let's look at some of the most notable offenders in the game today:

1. **TikTok:** As one of the fastest-growing social media platforms in the world, TikTok is a video editing and sharing platform that allows users to create stories with music, filters, trimmed clips, stickers, and text. TikTok videos can be entertaining, informative, creepy, or inappropriate, making it a seriously addictive social media app. That's what sets it apart from so many other social media sites today— TikTok is primarily entertaining, versus a lifestyle experience.

Filling the void that was left by Vine after Twitter shut it down, TikTok is the perfect place for users to express themselves creatively, without all of the pressure to "look perfect" that can come with Instagram. That is why the app has five hundred million active users as of right now, ranking it as the ninth most popular social network—surpassing the likes of LinkedIn, Twitter, Snapchat, and Pinterest.[23] Additionally, forty-one percent of TikTok users are between the ages of thirteen and sixteen, which makes it the most popular Gen Z social media app in existence today.[24]

Even more impressive, fifty-six percent of TikTok users are male, which completely goes against the typically female-centered usage stats for sites like Instagram and Snapchat.[25] On average, users of the app spend about fifty-two minutes on it every day, looping through video after video. When one opens the app, it immediately starts playing video reels, which can make it easy to waste a lot of time going through the content.

Cons of TikTok: Since the app is based on entertainment, if a teen wants to have a popular account, they need to be entertaining. This requires the user to continually push themselves to find new, more drastic ways of creating entertainment. This can cause teens to dump buckets of water on their parents and film it, spray graffiti at their school with a mask on and edit it, or engage in cyberbullying to get a laugh out of their classmates. During the rise of the coronavirus, there are kids posting videos claiming to have it or making fun of those who do. Such actions will backfire in the long term. On top of that, many users create even more bizarre and sexually charged videos to satisfy this desire for increased entertainment. When you talk to your child about TikTok, look to ensure they are not exploiting humans for their own personal follower count.

Otherwise, the app is harmless. Not to beat a dead horse, but it is how the app is used, other than some security issues with apps themselves, that makes an app dangerous. These mediums can be an excellent place for teens to find their personal creative voice and identity, just as long as it does not turn into a *Lord of the Flies* situation.

As the tagline states, TikTok's mission is to "capture and present the world's creativity, knowledge, and precious life moments, directly from the mobile phone." The app is three years old to date and was created in China. Of course, a Chinese app is capturing more than creativity when it comes to your child's data.

2. **Instagram:** We have to, of course, touch on Instagram next, which captures the age range of eighteen to twenty-nine better than any other app.[26] About sixty-four percent of Instagram users fall into this age range, which means older teens in the seventeen- to twenty-year-old range will be captivated by Instagram more than any other social media site.[27]

    Instagram has gone mainstream in recent years after Facebook acquired it and added it to its growing empire. Instagram is a simple photo and video sharing app, with an Instagram Stories feature, IGTV where videos can be edited and posted, and an Instagram Highlights feature on profiles that organizes all past Instagram Stories. As the fastest-growing social media site in the world, with over one billion users, Instagram is a big place.[28] Your teen will spend a lot of time on this app, looking at other people's photos and video posts.

However, Instagram comes with some negatives. Among the various social media sites, it has been proven to cause the most depression and anxiety in teens since Instagram is a "beauty" contest. Photos of girls in bikinis are posted to show off bodies, luxurious homes to show off wealth, and private jets to show off travel abilities, along with anything else that inspires envy. Sitting on Instagram causes depression in users that feel their lives are not as cool as that of the person they are following.

As we all know, social media is an illusion, and that goes for the content curated on an Instagram feed. Be sure to talk to your teen about this phenomenon and the danger of daydreaming on Instagram for too long each day. If they understand that what they are seeing has been doctored and altered, they will realize it's silly to feel bad about posts.

Note: Instagram is considering removing likes from the platform to diminish the amount of influencer marketing that is occurring. With this metric gone, teens may feel less pressure to look and appear a certain way. It should be interesting to see what happens!

YouTube: Did you know that YouTube is the second largest search engine in the entire world today? In fact, five hundred hours of video are uploaded to YouTube every single minute, with over one billion hours of videos watched on YouTube every single day.[29] In any given month, eight out of ten eighteen- to forty-nine-year-olds will watch a video on YouTube.[30]

YouTube is also a popular subculture for teens today, with many vloggers popularizing the concept of talking to a camera while sharing information about their personal lives.[ii] Teens will follow these icons, as well as consider vlogging themselves. The youngest famous vlogger to date, according to The Verge, was only five years old![31]

YouTube is an easy way to stay up-to-date on the latest pop culture, news, music videos, makeup tutorials, and everything else that is pertinent to teens. The social media app even has a movie subscription model, as well as a music model that enables users to watch movies and TV shows and listen to music without any ads or interruptions. Overall, YouTube isn't something you need to worry too much about for your teen. A *60 Minutes* feature in December 2019 noted that the social media app could not possibly remove all sensitive content immediately after posting.[iii] So teens can find porn, sex, death, violence, terrorist information, conspiracy theories, and other kinds of content on the site before it is removed.[32,33] Then again, they can find that information on Facebook and Google as well if they want to look for it.

3. **Snapchat:** Last but not least, we have Snapchat, which used to reign supreme in the world of teen social media usage. In recent years, Snapchat has taken a serious engagement hit after Instagram adopted Instagram Stories, which

---

[ii] A *vlogger* is a video blogger.

[iii] YouTube uses a mix of an automated machine learning flagging of material, and manual flags. This can lead to sensitive content being on YouTube for extensive periods.

embedded the Snapchat business model right into the app. Most individuals over the age of twenty-one do not use Snapchat anymore, but that doesn't mean your teen isn't using it.

Due to the fact that adults are off of Snapchat, teens love to use it for the inappropriate message and imagery exchanges that you, as a parent, cannot monitor. When a Snap is sent, it can be up to ten seconds in length. The user will open the Snap and have ten seconds to watch it before it disappears forever. Although there is a "replay" option, the recipient can only replay the Snap once before it is gone.

Be sure to tell your teen that smartphones can still take screenshots of Snaps, and there are apps designed to permanently capture these images, which is why risqué pictures and videos can end up permanent without your teen realizing it.

Since the basic premise of Snapchat is fleeting content, it's where teens feel most comfortable sending information and imagery they know is not appropriate. Typically, users will send provocative or suggestive photos and videos, as well as silly content they don't want to exist forever.

In total, eighty-three percent of users on Snapchat are teens.[34] This platform gives them a personal messaging haven that they can't find on any other app today. Additionally, the overall layout and design of Snapchat can be so complex and difficult to navigate that it scares away adults, especially those your age. You don't need to be a master at using it to talk to your teen about it; you just need to explain that screenshots could ruin their future lives forever.

Lesser-Known Teen Social Sites

This is where it can be hard to keep an exact beat on what your teen is up to online. They will continually engage in brand-new social media sites that they feel are hidden from your oversight. The pace at which they will do this will be frustrating for you, which is why you need to commit to a lifelong investment in learning about social media sites, as opposed to ignoring them.

Here is a brief overview of some lesser-known teen social sites on your teen's phone:

- **GroupMe:** This is a free messaging app that doesn't charge for group or direct messages. Teens can send gifs, emojis, and videos, planning for meetups that they want to hide from you.

- **Kik Messenger:** Also, a free messaging app, Kik is fast, has no message limits, character limits, or fees, and can be used easily through any smartphone. However, stranger danger is a severe issue on Kik, since users simply have a username for chatting and that's it. This anonymity has led to it being a communication mechanism for the Bondage/ Dominance/Sadism/Masochism (BDSM) community and those conducting illicit activities. The app has been connected to high-profile crimes, like the murder of a thirteen-year-old girl, as well as a child pornography case.[35]

- **WhatsApp:** Owned by Facebook, WhatsApp is the world's most popular "free" messaging tool that enables users to text and call people around the world, with no roaming charges or plans required. Of note, WhatsApp's cofounders left the firm over arguments with the parent company over data privacy issues with what Facebook was implementing.[36] I believe there will be more extensive data fallout with Facebook's use of user information as they push to find new ways to monetize these users' data.

- **Discord:** First founded as a place for gamers to chat while they game, Discord has become a popular platform where users can text, voice chat, and video chat privately.

- **Tumblr:** Tumblr used to be much bigger than it is today, although it is still relatively popular among teens. It's a basic blogging platform whereby users can share photos, posts, videos, boards, and anything else aesthetic to their profile. It's a place where a teen typically will express intimate information about their personality. As mentioned, Tumblr's use is on the decline because they started censoring adult content.

- **Houseparty:** This group video chat app is a way for teens to video call each other all at once, enabling two to eight people to use the app at once. Chats can be locked so no one else can join, or they can be left public for anyone to see. If public, the teens will get a notification if someone else joins the chat. If it is someone they don't know, they can leave the chat. It's important to note that screenshots can be taken during the chat session, so the activity is not as private as your kids might think.

- **Live.me:** Live.me is growing in prominence quickly. It's a live video streaming app that enables kids to watch others and broadcast themselves live. It's one of the most accessible places for kids to see inappropriate content like live sex, food porn, and anything else that has a "fetish" community online.

- **Whisper:** This confessional app allows users to post what is on their mind, paired with an image. It ends up being a massive source of cyberbullying as teens anonymously (but still clearly) bully someone.

- **Monkey:** The Monkey app provides something known as *roulette video chatting*, where users are paired with strangers and have ten seconds to chat with them before moving on to the next user.

- **Yubo:** This the new Tinder for teens. If you have banned Tinder from your teen's phone, they may download Yubo to access the same kind of content and pairing. To use the app, teens have to share their personal information and location, which can put them at risk for predators and offenders utilizing the app.

- **Amino:** Last but not least, there's Amino, which is known for community chats, forums, and groups. It's an interest-based marketplace that lets users find people who are into the same things as they are. Contacting strangers is part of the experience, which is why mature content and bullying can run rampant on the app. The app was not made with kids in mind, which is why having your teen on it can be bad for their mental health.

Don't Take Away the Phone

After reading all of that, you probably want to take away your teen's phone. In fact, some sixty-five percent of parents have taken their teen's cellphone or internet privileges away as punishment.[37] Additionally, about fifty-five percent of parents will reduce screen time for their teen as a form of punishment.[38]

We want to stress that this is not the answer. Your teen will still find a way onto all of these apps. There is no stopping it. The best way is to educate them about being safe on the internet and make them aware of the downside of these apps. Discussions and conversations are much more important than just trying to make it all go away.

Should You Check Your Teen's Internet History?

This is a question every parent asks themselves daily. You want to respect and cherish your teen, which is why you probably do not want to invade their personal space and information. It can feel wrong to check their social media usage, like a total breach of trust. Worse, if they were to find out that you were checking on what they were doing and saying online, they would be much more likely to rebel against you.

Stats show the following:

- 61% of parents say they have checked the websites their teens have visited.[39]

- 60% have checked their teen's social media profiles.[40]

- 56% have friended or followed their teen on social media.[41]

- 48% have looked through their teen's phone, texts, or call records.[42]

Nearly half of parents know the password to their teen's email accounts as well.[43]

This can get tricky. We believe that you need to do what's necessary to keep your child safe today. There is a lot of potential for harm online, which is why checking in on their social media sites and website visits is not necessarily a bad thing. We just ask that you be stealthy about it, or else you will upset your teen and cause them to distance themselves from you even more. Start with a basic search of their name in Google to see what is publicly available about them. This is a good starting point for a search and something you even should do for yourself.

If you are considering looking at your teen's internet accounts, know that you are not alone. You are just doing what needs to be done to keep your kid protected. We completely get it.

After reading the next chapter, you are going to want to check their accounts even more. But remember, communication with their peers is vital for your children. Building trust, not always an easy task with this age group, is the best way to give your children a channel to talk about these problems.

Now it's time to explore the psychological impacts of social media use today.

Chapter 3

The Psychological Impact of Social Media

*The reason we struggle with insecurity is because we
compare our behind-the-scenes with everyone else's
highlight reel.* [44]
—Steven Furtick

When we devote just minutes of our day to something, day after day, that something becomes a habit.[45] Well, imagine when we do that something two to three hours each day, and it's social media. Our world has become obsessed with social media. Neither you nor I can put the phone down, look up, or unplug from the buzzing digital world that draws us in so easily. This same effect is happening to your teen, except that at their formidable age, psychological side effects are highly probable by the time they reach adulthood.

When we are in our teens, our bodies and brains are still growing. We are malleable. What we see, observe, and feel can impact us for the rest of our lives. That's why social media can be so impactful on young teens—they don't know any better. The more they consume on social media, the more it can change their personality, thoughts, and beliefs forever.

Not to mention, social media has been linked to causing severe depression and sadness in users. Teens are more depressed, anxious, and suicidal today than ever before. We do not believe it is a coincidence but rather a side effect of social media usage. We are not in the present anymore. I bet that at some point since you started reading this book, you had to pause to check your social media—be honest! The same thing happens with your teen.

In order to be the best parent for your teen, it is essential to understand the psychological impacts of social media. With this kind of information, you can better help your teen identify psychological problems and help your teen support their friends that need psychological support. Social media is a world of mental engagement, with nothing physical or tangible to show for it. It's a kind of warfare that is entirely new.

We're going to take some time to get psychological on you here, going deep into the psyche, so you know exactly what you are dealing with. But first, below is a general list of what social media is doing to you and your kid, right now.

The Top 6 Psychological Side Effects of Social Media

#1: Social Media Is Highly Addictive

Do you know what your child's average screen time is? It's an easy number you can retrieve from their phone's settings. Chances are, it is more than seven hours on any given day.[46] Just think about that for a minute. That is a LOT of time to be staring at a phone, most likely on social media. In five hours, something could be built, you could drive to another state, or you could run a marathon. That is a lot of time wasted on liking, commenting, and pinning posts. That is because social media is highly addictive, and no one can say otherwise.

If you looked at your phone right now and saw eleven missed notifications on your Facebook, could you shut off the phone and look at the notifications tomorrow? Probably not. You want to know what's going on, who said what, who commented on your photo, or if your post is doing well. This is all due to the reasons we provided at the beginning of this book. We just cannot get enough!

Beyond being something that is obviously popular in our lives, social media has been proven to be a real addiction, one comparable to smoking cigarettes or gambling.

Scientists who have studied social media usage have found that "addiction disorders" apply to teens today. Given that neglect of personal life, mental preoccupation, escapism, mood modifying experiences, tolerance, and concealing of the addiction are occurring. Additionally, there is a withdrawal period that comes if social media sites are taken away. One study found people experienced the psychological symptoms of withdrawal when they stopped using social media apps.[47] Mixed feelings of anxiety, depression, lack of interest, and irritability were witnessed in the test studies.

Therefore, taking away your child's phone or forcing them to delete social media apps is not the answer at the end of the day. Although it may sound silly, you will be plunging them into a depression that can make any psychological side effects worse.

#2 It's More Negative Than Positive

Countless studies have found the more a person uses social media, the less happy they become. One particular study found that Facebook was linked to both less moment-to-moment happiness and less life satisfaction.[48] The more the test subjects used

Facebook, the less happy and satisfied they felt by the end of the day.

This is because, at the end of the day, nothing can compare to the actual satisfaction of spending time with people in person. We were designed to laugh, feel, touch, smile, and cry. None of that is satisfied by using social media. It ends up tricking all of us into thinking that we are "connecting" more than ever before when, in reality, we are actually more isolated today than ever before.

However, this doesn't actually mean you are isolated. In fact, social media helps us create a perception in our own minds that we are isolated. You can still easily go next door, tap on your neighbor's door, and say hello to them. You can set up a time to get coffee with a friend. You can do a lot of things that can break the isolationism. But you do not, because you could also just sit at home by the fireplace with your laptop open, telling yourself you are getting in your "socializing," when it is just not the same thing.

Social media, therefore, becomes a negative entity in our lives that is tearing all of us apart without even realizing it.

#3 The Eternal Comparing

Sure, one could make the argument that comparing ourselves to one another is innate. It is what breeds competition and a desire to do more or succeed. That kind of comparison can be healthy until it becomes something that happens in your mind every single day.

It is impossible not to compare when someone in your Facebook feed posts about their new car or how their kids got into the University of Michigan. (Let's be honest, Harvard is overrated.) You then sit and think about how your kids only got into community colleges, or about how you don't have the money to get a new car.

You then start to feel frustrated and sorry for yourself. You convince yourself that your life is terrible and that this person on Facebook has the perfect life you are never going to have.

You start to make judgments about yourself, or against others, so there is a final verdict in the one-on-one comparison. And let's say you are the one posting about the new car. You may also feel bad about posting it and causing any strife in those that view it. This is known as comparison in both the upward and downward direction. Typically, only downward comparisons can make us feel poorly, but not in the world of social media.

This is the concept of "Keeping up with the Joneses" on steroids.[iv] Of course, this kind of perpetual comparison is strongly linked with depression. We convince ourselves that we will never have what we want and, worse, tell ourselves we are not worthy of what that other person has. A slew of negative mental emotions can start to take over your mind when you compare yourself to the fairy tales on social media.

#4 Rotten Jealousy

Comparing ourselves to others leads to jealousy. When we see someone on a tropical vacation in the Caribbean, and we are stuck home shoveling snow, we become jealous of them and their idyllic lifestyle. Jealousy is a nasty feeling, which causes us to become mean, depressed, anxious, and vindictive. This jealousy can create a vicious cycle in which we start to post content that we know will make people envious of our lives.

[iv] *Keeping up with the Joneses* is a comic strip of the McGinis family that is trying to "keep up" with the life style of their neighbors, the Jones family.

This then inundates social media with content that is not accurate or reflective of a person's actual life. As we do this, we contribute to a social media newsfeed that is unreal, envious, negative, and jealous, which sets a seriously terrible tone for our days.

From this jealously, we start to hate those people. We want to unfriend them or look away. We don't want to ask them to coffee anymore, when a few years ago, they were our good friends. You cannot bear to be around their positivity that is apparent on social media (even though those images do not paint a valid picture whatsoever).

#5: False Positives

This is the same kind of psychological concept that gets drug addicts to continue taking drugs. We tell ourselves that getting a fix is going to make everything better. This goes back to a psychological problem in the human brain that prevents us from understanding that the forecast is incorrect. We sign onto Facebook thinking it's going to make it all better, when in reality, it makes it worse.

One study articulated how people think they're going to feel after using Facebook, versus how they really feel. They think it is going to make them feel better because they are engaging with friends and family who love them. In reality, the comparisons and jealousy just make them feel worse, which means what we think is different from the reality we live in.

This is a very typical side effect regarding something that is addictive, which in social media's case has been proven time and time again. None of us want to admit that social media is not good for our mental health, so we tell ourselves lies to justify our usage of it day after day.

#6 Friend Disillusion

Numbers, lists, and bullets make it easier for our brains to understand ephemeral concepts. Quantity is easier to measure than quality. That is why I am writing these points in a list right now. Well, the same thing holds true for social media, which creates these numerical values that are supposed to assign worth to our social presence. We look for follower counts, friends, likes, comments, shares, retweets, etc., to gauge how popular something was or was not.

The same thing holds true with social media. When we sign on online and see twenty-three hundred Facebook friends, we think we are pretty social. However, this number of social media friends does not necessarily mean you have a better social life. There is actually a cap on the number of friends a person's brain can handle, requiring actual social interaction to fulfill that burning desire in our hearts to be liked and heard.[49] Renowned British anthropologist Robin Dunbar calculated that a person can only maintain about one hundred and fifty social friendships.[50]

Since Facebook, or rather overall extensive social media use, has been linked to depression, serial jealousy, and unhappiness, getting real social interaction is the healthiest option for both you and your teen.

These are just some of the most significant ways in which social media is impacting your teen's sense of reality (and probably yours as well). It is now time for us to look at the more personal, emotional elements of social media usage and what it can be doing to your teen right now.

Emotional Side Effects of Social Media Usage

- **Lower Self-Esteem:** We all have insecurities, no matter how good-looking or talented we might be. Some of us are willing to speak about them out loud, others are not. Well, one look at someone's perfectly curated Instagram feed can force us to face these insecurities head-on. Maybe your teen is overweight. Looking at the other skinny girls in their school parading around in a bikini on Instagram will cause them to face their body image issues daily.

  It then makes it nearly impossible for that person to build up self-esteem and feel confident or beautiful. This constant state of comparison with teens around the world will always ensure there is a teen that is prettier, skinnier, smarter, or funnier. Competing with the worldwide market is not easy, and it is going to make self-doubt much more likely than self-esteem.

  Dr. Tim Bono, author of *When Likes Aren't Enough*, tells us, "When we derive a sense of worth based on how we are doing in comparison to others, we are placing our happiness in a variable that is completely beyond our control."[51]

  If you are conscious of these kinds of comparisons, you and your child should spend less time scrolling through newsfeeds. With this new time returned, teens can work on themselves and their own self-confidence, refining what they love about themselves.

- **Loneliness:** Even though we are more connected than ever before, with transportation options at all of our fingertips, loneliness is at an all-time high. It's so essential for us to be able to communicate and create personal relationships with other people in our lives. When we are glued to our screens, it becomes hard to bond with people in person, looking at their mannerisms, intonation, and other personal characteristics that can't come through a phone.

Social media also fuels what is known as FOMO: fear of missing out. If we see a video posted of three of our closest friends hanging out, we feel like we have been left out. In reality, the friends may have run into each other at the store or were assigned to a school project together. Whatever the reason, the imagery of the people hanging out together can cause the viewer to feel like they were personally isolated and left out of the equation.

This can create rifts in friendships for no reason, as well as make the person with FOMO feel incredibly depressed.

- **Memory Distortion:** Yes, social media can be an easy way to reminisce when you are back with all of your friends. In just a few scrolls, you can see some of your content that was published ten years ago. It is like your own personal scrapbook, right in your pocket.

Social media is, therefore, great for looking back fondly on memories and reflecting on the past. But it can distort how we reflect on the past as well as what we remember from certain portions of our life.[52] In any given picture, the visual marvel we are looking at might have taken an hour to curate, and everyone was actually fighting that day. But the photo is gorgeous, and it looked like the perfect place for a picture—so we forget how much of a hassle it was.

From the picture, we remember the very best of our memory and our life, skewing our perception of reality into thinking "how good everything used to be." This puts pressure on us to continue the goodness, or else we feel bad for what our lives look like in the present compared to the past. When we do this, we're comparing ourselves with ourselves!

- **Poor Sleep:** Our bodies rely on sleep more than you realize. That is why engaging in activities like social media that can contribute to insomnia is not something you want to do to your body. The body needs sleep, especially in teenagers, to aid its growth and development.

  Here is where phones and other electronic devices can be a problem. If you use your phone up until you sleep, it can completely impact your sleep schedule and sleeping ability. When we stare at bright white or blue light screens, it actually tricks our brains into thinking that it is sunny out. Deep down, we think the sun is about to rise, with the brain communicating to the body that it's time to get up and start the day.

  This can alter your ability to finally close your eyes, as well as diminish the quality of REM sleep you are able to get that night. The basic science behind this is that the blue wavelengths of light emitted from these devices stimulate certain neurological functions in the brain. This altered neurological function makes you think it is daytime and prevents your mind from entering a sleep state.

  Plus, social media can inspire anxiety in teens, which is why checking one's phone to see a party they weren't invited to will kickstart them awake for another hour as they wrestle with their crippling anxiety.

  Teach your teen to put down the phone at least one hour before bed and read a book or talk to you. All options are better than burying their face in their smartphone as they fall asleep.

- **Attention Spans:** The average human attention span is eight seconds today, down from twelve seconds in the year 2000. Where is it going to be just five years from now? That is a scary thought. With social media, we have become accustomed to having everything we want in the palm of our hands. That is why so many of us end up just reading headlines as opposed to entire articles—if we can distill the information in just a few seconds, we will.

  The more time your teen spends on social media, the shorter their natural attention span will be. People become easily distracted when they bury themselves in their social accounts, which means they are less likely to be present in person. This can be a terrible trait of a teen that grows up to have no social skills, no ability to communicate, and no ability to collaborate in a work setting.

  Although it is okay if your teen is on social media, try to build non-social-media-related activities into their days and weekends, so they see that life is fun without their phones.

- **Anxiety:** One in twenty US teens live with crippling anxiety or depression today.[53] That's right, more kids are living with anxiety, depression, PTSD, and suicidal thoughts than ever before in our history, and social media can be a contributing factor, according to research.[54]

  Social media promotes anxiety in a number of ways. Kids are stressed out about their content and if they look "good" or are "popular" with other teens on social media; they are anxious about cyberbullying, afraid they are either going to be a victim or accidentally end up on the side of the bully;

and they are fed propaganda that anxiety is normal and cool, causing them to adopt the characteristics of being anxious.

Anxiety is such a common side effect of social media that teens are actually aware of it. In March 2018, a study was done on one thousand Gen Z teens stating they were quitting social media.[55] Close to 41 percent admitted that social platforms make them feel anxious, sad, or depressed.[56] The study found that students that left social media became happier, as well as those that took a hiatus. You do not necessarily need to quit social media for good—you just need to be aware of its link to anxiety and other mental-health-related problems.

Suicide

One of the worst and most unthinkable side effects of social media today is suicidal thoughts or tendencies. Due to the aggressive comparisons, bullying, and cyberbullying, like catfishing, that occurs on social sites, teens can end up retreating into dark, dark mental places, convincing themselves the world would just be better off without them in it.

That is why suicide is at an all-time high among teens—especially LGBT teens.[57] We have seen instances where other teens have convinced their friends or boyfriends to kill themselves; we have seen gay students "outed" on social media who elected to kill themselves thereafter, and we've just seen cyberbullying victims choose suicide instead of telling their parents.

There was an entire Netflix series called *13 Reasons Why* dedicated to this kind of invisible bullying that parents don't understand. Invisible bullying is such a new thing in our world that it can be incredibly frustrating and challenging to comprehend. Unfortunately, the repercussions can be devastating, and in the case of suicide, permanent.

Here are a few ways to tell if your teen is being cyberbullied online:

- **They exhibit a skittishness when they open their phone or receive a notification.**

- **They pull away from their friends and social situations.**

- **They ask to skip school frequently.**

- **Teachers report that they skip class frequently.**

- **They've lost interest in things that once made them happy.**

- **They sleep a lot or exhibit depressive tendencies.**

- **They exhibit aggressive mood swings and outbursts.**

- **They operate as a loner.**

- **They start to starve themselves or overeat.**

- **They hurt themselves.**

More schools are putting systems in place to ensure that parents are made aware of any changes in mood or habits, as this can be an indicator of online bullying. Teachers are also tasked with the job of detecting these kinds of side effects, so we recommend that you work closely with the educators at your school to ensure kids are receiving the help they need.

If your school is not yet set up with any kind of whistleblower system related to cyberbullying, we suggest that you create one, or reach out to us at Security Squad. It will enable kids to anonymously report cyberbullying, as well as tip-off teachers to students that might be in danger and need some help. A cyberbullying whistleblower program needs to be in place, an education system needs to be established to teach the students and teachers, and the school needs to communicate this policy to parents. It is an atrocity that many schools do not see this program within their "budget" or school initiatives. The worst thing you can do is ignore these signs. I even have had conversations with school principals who claim to be on the frontier of childhood education but have said that they had no cyberbullying policies in place, and they would instead take their chances.

Are There Other Side Effects?

As you can imagine, there are a variety of other side effects of frequent social media usage. The ones I've listed here are just the massive indicators that social media is wreaking havoc on your teen's mental health and stability.

Having a conversation with your teen about what social media can do to their health is important. If they are aware of the psychological side effects, they are more likely to remove themselves personally from conversations that concern them, their appearance, and their popularity on social media.

Remember: mental health issues are not something that can be "scolded" away. They need to be handled with delicate care. If your teen is anxious, depressed, or suicidal, then it's not their fault. They need professional help immediately and for you to be an understanding parent. Today's kids don't have it easy, and we need to be cognizant of that.

Now it is time to approach teen social media from a new angle—from the teen's point of view, as well as what they do not understand today.

Chapter 4

What Your Teen Doesn't Understand

Knowledge is power, and in this case, knowledge is the ability to understand how social media will shape one's life. First, teens are classified as kids ages thirteen to nineteen.[58] Our teenage years are some of our most impressionable and can set the stage for the rest of our lives. Although a lot of child-rearing impressions occur during our younger years, our teens are when we learn if we are going to sink or fly, if we can get along with others, if we can communicate properly, if we are desirable, etc.

That is why teens are so sensitive—they do not know who they are or what they want. All they know is that their bodies are changing rapidly, and there is nothing they can do about it. They often feel out of control and lost, and yearn for the days when they are older, sure about themselves, and set in their ways.

The problem is that during our teen years, we do not know what we do not know. That is why teens are so frustrated and often rude. Teens have yet to go out into the world and experience what it's like firsthand. They do not know how hard it is to work a job and pay bills. They do not know much about actual reality, which means they think they know everything about their little enclave.

This sense of self-inflated assuredness can get teens in trouble online. Obviously, a twenty-nine-year-old adult knows not to send personal information and images to a predator online. It goes without saying. However, a teen has not yet experienced that much life, hardship, or genuine danger. They do not know what is really out there in the real world, so they are willing to test the waters in the meantime.

In their minds, they think: "What could go wrong?"

We were all teens once, which means we all had minds that functioned in a similar manner.

The problem is that there is a lot your teen does not know. Too much. In fact, we shelter them from not knowing, because the world out there is dark, brutal, and unbearable at times, especially today.

This is a chapter that challenges you to see things from your teen's perspective, so you can better understand why they do what they do online.

What Your Teen Doesn't Understand About Social Media

Problem 1: Real Stranger Danger

In reality, sometimes the perpetrator is not a stranger—and kids let their guard down, placing themselves in danger. This sadly sums everything up perfectly. There is a twofold problem when it comes to the internet and your teenager's access to the internet:

- **The "stranger" is not always a stranger to the teen.** Did you know that a child or teen is more likely to be abused by someone they know than a totally random person?[59] That is why the stranger in stranger danger might not always be a stranger. This can be confusing to teens. It can be someone they have chatted with for a long time through one of the anonymous texting apps that are popular today, or it can be someone pretending to be someone else. It can even be who the person says they are, after they have spent months winning the teen's affection and adoration.

  Once the stranger is no longer a stranger, they are more likely to get the teen to submit to coming over, engaging in inappropriate activities, etc.

- **Teens know they are in danger.** The problem is that since the teen thinks this "stranger" is their friend or virtual lover, they do not sense any real danger. Communicating through phones and texting eliminates an in-person element that can make it easier for us to detect problems, mannerisms, eye movements, etc. When we do not have that kind of exposure, we cannot fully get a read on someone. Since we are not in person with the person, we do not experience the same sense of danger that we should.

  This leads teens to send inappropriate content, images, and videos, and even worse, meet up with the internet friend in person. Although attacks/deaths via these kinds of meetups are rare, they are still something that can happen—and something you should be starkly aware of today.

Predators know that they can access just about any kind of student through social media. It is a place where they can find the target they are looking for, typically girls that appear quieter and more self-conscious.[60] These girls are looking for someone to provide them with compliments and validation that they do not otherwise get at school.

It is the perfect opportunity for a predator to swoop in and convince the girl that they are there for them through it all.

Therefore, please talk with your teen about stranger danger. They may roll their eyes and look the other way, but they will hear you. Talk about how this can happen through social media easily since no one really knows who is operating the other account.

Additionally, if you notice your child talking on their phone the entire day to one particular name or username, ask them about it (nicely). You do want to find out more, but you do not want to embarrass them in the process as this will only scare them away.

Problem 2: Identifying an Addiction Problem

Children likely will not have an "addiction" experience like adults do. Maybe they know a family member who is struggling with some addiction, but there may still be a cognitive disconnect of what addiction really means. They are not aware of what alcohol, drugs, and gambling can do to us over time. Although some teens will experiment with recreational drugs and alcohol, during their younger teen years, we are not familiar with addiction versus moderation.

Therefore, teens won't understand that they need to take a break from social media. They do not know how to identify if they are spending too much time doing one singular thing.

It is up to you to step in and explain why taking social media breaks is so important. Your teen, over time, will start to see how much better they feel when they put their phone down. We are not saying force them to throw their phone in a basket every day when they get home from school. Just maybe set aside a time window each day, on vacation, and during the holidays to help your teen adjust to reasonable screen time. Get them involved in sports and have cell phone-free family dinners. This is just a start, but this is where it starts.

As we mentioned above, social media is actually an addictive tendency in our world today. Teens go through withdrawal if they are forced to quit it cold turkey. Be reasonable and moderate in how you approach this topic, letting them know that phone addictions are real problems.

Problem 3: The Permanence of Social Media

This is a big one, and it is one that most people still are trying to fully comprehend. When we post content to the internet, it is there forever. One hard-to-swallow truth is that everything online is permanent. Yes, everything. Yes, even if it is set to private or promptly deleted. Everything. Even on private account settings with limited connections, screenshots and screen recordings can be saved and resurface years later. Additionally, systems around the world are archiving websites and social media platforms in their entirety, and in real-time. The collected and stored data is not currently being utilized to its full potential, but advanced AI technology is being invented to turn the overwhelmingly complex task into realistic processing.

Unfortunately, if any of us had been given access to social media in our younger years, we would have been in the same kind of trouble. Can you imagine if there was documentation of what you did after you got out of school each day? It is a frightening thought.

These poor kids today are going through the same sense of adventure and rebellion, except in their world, it's documented.

When pictures of teens making out, drinking, doing drugs, or committing crimes grace the internet, the pictures live on forever. This can haunt your teen in a variety of ways:

- **College Applications:** About twenty-five percent of colleges will check an applicant's social media before admitting them to the university.[61] Although that may not seem like a lot, it is still about one-fourth of institutions that are considering your teen at graduation. This figure will only increase in size, scale, and invasiveness as schools look for any blemish on a student's record. Advances in big data and AI will make this nearly automatic for them. You do not want anything working against your children, especially in today's world where competition to get into elite schools is mounting.

- **Job Applications:** After college, about seventy percent of potential employers will screen someone's social media before hiring a candidate today.[62] That's a lot of businesses. If there is just one photo that has lingered from those teen years, depicting your kid funneling a beer or doing a handstand in the backyard naked, they are probably going to pass them up for the other candidate.

  You might be thinking to yourself: "Yes, but my teen will just delete the photo or tweet." Well, it's not that easy. What if someone else owns the photo? Even if your teen un-tags themselves, the photo will still be online. The same goes for videos and timeline posts. Again, as I mentioned above, there are time machines archiving everything online.

Additionally, what if one of their friends posts the photo again, five years later, right on their profile? You can bet the employer is going to see this content and think again. Or what if there was a data breach, as is a common phenomenon, and all of those images are posted to the dark web.

- **Dating:** Let's be honest, we all look up our potential date's social media before we actually go meet them. It is an excellent way for us to vet them ahead of time, deciding if they are right for us or not. They like dogs? Great, we have something in common! But they may have photos or messages that are less innocent than that. If the date sees that you were a total degenerate for ten years of your life, they may judge you before they even meet you. This same thing holds true for new networking partners and friends; first impressions are lasting impressions.

  Tenant Selection: In order for you to get a particular apartment or house, you can bet the landlord will be doing some social media vetting. If the landlord sees you are a party animal, they are going to go with the applicant that appears responsible and clean.

- **Arrests:** Many times, teens will engage in illegal activities, only to never get caught. The problem today is that if that activity is filmed and posted somewhere, it can make its way back to the police. We have seen this dozens of times with parties in abandoned homes. The media from the party helps the cops make the appropriate arrests, when, otherwise, the teen would have gotten away with it.

Make sure your teen understands that under no circumstances is it ever okay to send explicit photos or other forms of content that will haunt them forever.

Problem 4: Underdeveloped Communication Skills

> *Social media is a convenient way of communicating, but it lessens the quality of the connection.*[63]
> *—Thrive Global*

Before social media, in order to connect, we called one another via the phone, grabbed a drink or a cup of coffee, and sat in person to strengthen the relationship. When we spent this kind of in-person time together, we were getting to know the other person's intonation, vocal inflections, mannerisms, reactions, facial features, etc. Although it is not something that we consciously think about, it is actually incredibly crucial for developing close, quality bonds with people.

Today, we simply stare at a screen with a keyboard. Sure, we can write to one another, but that is all we can do. It is akin to receiving letters in the past. It is a great start, but it is not the whole shebang.

Unfortunately, communicating through phones and laptops is more comfortable than doing it in person. It requires less energy and fewer communication skills. You really do not need any skills at all to write a message. So when teens that spend the majority of their days communicating through phones have to look someone in the eye and talk with them, they struggle. And it is not going to change anytime soon—74 percent of millennials prefer conversing digitally, as opposed to in person.[64]

Technology is not going anywhere, but neither is the need to communicate with other humans. It is a fundamental skill we need to date, to get a new job, to teach, and to make new friends. Teens will not realize they are stunting their natural communication skills by spending so much time on social media. It is up to you to make them talk out loud in person, at dinner, looking people in the eye. These simple communication skills will make them so much more valuable to companies looking to hire, etc.

Problem 5: Life Isn't a Popularity Contest

Social media is based on popularity. Who has more followers? Who received more likes on their profile picture? Who has the most engagement? These are all questions teens are asking each other when they get together and go over the different profiles of kids in their grade. These metrics teach teens that everything is a popularity contest, from their bikini pics to their entertaining videos on TikTok.

Children do not realize that in the grand scheme of things, life is not a popularity contest. Once you get out of school, life becomes this big, stressful whirlwind of emotions that requires jobs, paid bills, and fortified relationships. How "popular" you once were on Instagram will do nothing for the success and true happiness of your life.

So although the popularity contest can seem like the entire world to your teen, try to show them that in a few years, they will look back on this time and laugh. It will lessen the pressure for your teen to appear hot, handsome, sexy, slim, or funny on social media every single day.

Start a Conversation

In the coming chapters, we will look at how you can be proactive as a parent in helping your teen understand what they do not know.

No typical teen wants to be told they are naïve or immature, which is why you want to make all of this more of a conversation than a one-way disciplining stance. You do not want them to rebel against you—you want them to feel like they can tell you if they are being cyberbullied, etc.

Chapter 5

Online Privacy Policies

*Don't say anything online that you wouldn't want plastered
on a billboard with your face on it.*[65]
—Erin Bury

We cannot just talk about the online privacy world for social media
websites/apps without dissecting parts of the privacy concerns at
large. In our increasingly digital world, there has been a lot of fear
and discussion about the negative physical, social, and emotional
impacts of living life in front of a screen, especially from parents.
How playing games will impact a child's learning, how extensive
digital interactions may change a child's perception of human
interaction. These concerns are endless, and I have discussed the
important ones in this book and other books. But the looming
question is, what data transfers are occurring through your Fitbit,
social media app, or child's video game? Data awareness and
conscious online privacy practices have been a quiet, less popular
thread of concern. The data collection, storage, sale, and
processing industry has grown exponentially over the past decade,
and governments and consumers are only just starting to catch up.

Understanding what all your kids' apps, social media platforms, and
devices are doing and sharing behind the scenes does not come

naturally. Personal data awareness is something that has to be taught, especially to groups that are at a higher risk of being victims of data theft and fraud, including seniors and children. In America, the average child receives their first cell phone at age ten.[66] Even though kids are growing up with devices, which may create the illusion that they are more adept with technology or aware of its influence, online privacy is not intuitive. Legal policies and data mining strategies are continually evolving, so consumers of all ages need to take a proactive step to understand their rights and safeguard their information.

Avoiding data-sharing entirely may seem impossible because, in today's world, it is. That is why this book is about teaching safe social media and online practices. Someone could break their phones and go live in a log cabin in the woods, but even then, there would still be a digital footprint of the person. Because when data is created online, it becomes impossible to destroy. For the rest of us to participate online, consumers have to trade data for access, but do you know how much you are really sharing? *Personal information* includes things like your name, phone number, address, email address, and social security number. Most consumers are cautious about typing in their social security number and pause before sharing their phone number, but that is just the tip of the iceberg. Do you know what you are giving to Google when you use their "free" Gmail service? Are you reading the fine print of their terms and conditions form? If you are reading it, do you understand what the jargon is really saying? Well, I will tell you I never read those agreements until recently, and I am continuously shocked by what I am giving them access to. You are entering into an agreement to provide your data to these various "free" services online, and some of this data is more private than you realize.

Personally identifiable information (PII) encompasses everything else, and that is driving the big data boom. Apple can recognize our faces, voices, work/sleep schedule, and fingerprints; Facebook can map our friendships, preferences, and life changes; Google can analyze our interests and follow our movements. Every day, we hand over our heart rate, step count, music preferences, relationship status, daily schedules, preferred activities, shopping habits, and more to be recorded. One piece of data may not be dangerous by itself, but when it is leaked and combined, companies and criminals can put the puzzle pieces together to target you with unparalleled accuracy.

Owing to the pervasive nature of the internet in today's digitized world, people have to be more aware and responsible for their data. Indeed, given the times we are in, observing security measures should become like second nature to us. This means that you should be cautious with all information related to your passwords, finances, health, sexual orientation, and biometric data at all times.

There most likely will be dire consequences to the loss of any, if not all, of your personal data. This is not limited to those hidden agreements you are signing online every time you access a new app or website. The wave of data theft is on the rise as new scams spring up every other day as cybercriminals keep hacking away in search of personal data. As the complexity of our devices continues, it becomes increasingly difficult to secure our personal data. Interestingly, when we carry out everyday tasks like making purchases, interacting with friends and loved ones, looking up things on Google, and whatnot, we run the risk of losing some of our personal data to third parties with less-than-pure intentions.

Besides the hackers who can use personal data to do terrible things, there is a breed of folks known as "data brokers" who have taken personal data theft to new heights. These folks have been known to mine and maintain data belonging to millions of people, which they process and sell without the owner's consent. While it appears as if everyone is at the mercy of data theft, that is not always the case. I say "theft" because the individuals who the data is about never consented to or weren't fully aware of what they were agreeing to when their data was created and thrown out there onto the dining table for the data brokers to feast on.

However, there is light at the end of the tunnel. The powers that be, in some cases, have set things in place to monitor and control the way personal data is used. The UK passed the Data Protection Act of 2018, which regulates how the personal data of users in the UK is used by the government and organizations within and outside the UK.[67] Personal data can only be legally used in compliance with the stipulations of the General Data Protection Regulation (GDPR). The operative word being "legally." There are a lot of unscrupulous elements who will not hesitate to harvest your personal data should you be so unaware of the security measures to take. Hence, being aware of your data involves knowing what constitutes your personal data, how much of it you are willing to divulge, who has access to it, why they have access to it, and how they use it. This is especially important because it powers the operations of the most profitable organizations in today's digitized business landscape. These digital companies (the Facebooks and Googles) gather and process your personal data into actionable insights that influence their business operations based on your needs and preferences.

While your personal data may not always be used for nefarious purposes, there is a need for stricter regulations for the use of personal data. The wave of data privacy scandals that have washed over us in recent times (the Google location tracking issues come to mind) point to the fact that there is still much to be desired with the way personal data is used with or without the owner's knowledge. However, there is only so much these regulations can do. The buck stops with the user and owner of the data. Protecting it starts with you and the steps you take to keep your personal data private.

It's now time for us to dive into some of these private data concerns. These big platforms do not necessarily want your teens to be in danger or to help foster any bullying. They are natural side effects of a massive, picture-posting, status-sharing, and private-messaging universe.

Therefore, here are some of the necessary privacy policy details that are included in most of the policies for major social sites today.

What Information Is Shared on Social Media?

This is a question about which teens do not have a clear answer. There are the obvious photos and videos that are posted to social media, but what about the not-so-obvious content and information that is aggregated each time a person signs onto one of these apps? When you sign up for a social media app, here is what you are sharing with that specific company:

1. **Your Profile:** When you set up a profile, you not only upload a photo and cover image, but you also release personal information, like your birthday, gender, age, familial relations, interests, educational background, and

employment. You do not have to fill these things out, which is why, if possible, recommend to your teen that they withhold all of this information. The fewer details you provide, the better.

2. **Your Status:** You can post status updates on sites like Facebook and Twitter, communicating your emotions, feelings, and opinions instantly. There are privacy settings that allow you to restrict access to status updates, which is why you want to make sure your teen's profiles are all set to the highest form of private.

3. **Your Location:** Many social media sites will request GPS access to your phone. "Would you like to share your location with X?" This can be for a status update or for longer-term tracking. It may ask to geotag our photos; this is when your photo contains metadata about its location. We need to ask ourselves what providing this information really means. GPS tracking is being used for location-based offers and focal clustering. By accessing geolocation data, marketers know who to target and where to source data for a more personalized strategy. Location-based marketing isn't new, but predictive algorithms are changing the game and making your option to share it that much more dangerous.

For example, by tracking daily travel patterns, marketers can send time- and location-based ads to entice an employee right before they leave for a lunch break. With behavioral and GPS data collected from a running app, marketers can suggest hiking boots after the user logs a new, scenic mountain course. The FBI also has used Fitbit location data to track criminals' movements and set perimeters for covert operations.

Continuous mapping and tracking are happening all the time, and most consumers are completely unaware. Consumer marketing is shifting toward individual profiles that take everything into account, from your purchase history and habits to your sleep schedule and daily routines. The feeling of distrust and concern over eerily targeted ads is growing, and many Americans may feel that they lack the control necessary to make independent decisions when browsing and shopping online.

4. **Shared Content:** Beyond your own content, you can share content on social media by reposting music, photos, videos, and links to other webpages. When you do this, social media sites can get an idea of your likes and dislikes, which will come into play later. With this, they create marketable profiles. To highlight this point, target marketing experts created scores that could predict if a woman were pregnant and when she was most likely to be due, simply based on the timing, amount, and kinds of items she was purchasing. In one example, a targeted coupon flyer was mailed to a sixteen-year-old girl with suggested discounts for diapers, maternity clothes, and other nursery essentials. Her father complained to a Target manager about the inappropriate advertising, but the family soon learned that she really was pregnant.[68]

With all of this information, social media sites, advertisers, marketers, and stalkers can get a thoroughly rounded picture of the user and what makes them tick. Between gender, age, and employment status, mixed with posts and status updates, anyone can know everything about you.

You are probably now wondering—what if my teen sets everything to private? Then they are protected from oversight, right?

Forever Public Information

Although you can restrict a person's ability to find your teen's social media page, there will always be a certain amount of public information that is accessible through the profile. This can include the username, the teen's name, and the teen's profile image.

We also want you to know:

- The account name and email address associated with the account will always be public.

- Approved contacts may copy and repost information from your account and share it with whomever they want. ANYTHING online is never truly private.

- Third-party apps that have paid the social media sites for advertising access will be granted the ability to view your private information.

- Cybercriminals can infiltrate the sites and break down any privacy barriers.

Social media sites do not guarantee any privacy to their users. Although they provide "privacy features" and switches, they are not liable if a marketing company or foreign government can access the user's profile. In July 2019, Facebook owed $5 billion in fines to the FTC for data mishandling, but the platform's shares were still up thirty-four percent from the previous year.[69] Despite the hefty penalty, Facebook's revenues have also increased by twenty-eight percent since 2018.[70] Similarly, Google was fined fifty-seven million dollars for violations after the GDPR was implemented in the EU earlier in 2019, but revenues continue to rise.[71] It appears that fines and penalties for inappropriate privacy practices are only a small price to pay amid this more significant data game. With the ever-pervasive nature of digitization, the world is at the point where openness, transparency, and less privacy will continue to mark our lives both online and offline.

Social media sites also do not guarantee the safety of the user, as well as the protection of private profiles. When a social media app is used, the user forfeits all rights to their personal information. The extent of personal information forfeiture varies by country and by state. New improvements with the European Union's General Data Protection Regulation (GDPR) and California's California Consumer Privacy Act (CCPR) now allow users to request the deletion of harvested personal data.[72] However, that does not stop providers from denying access if you do not agree to all of the privacy conditions in the first place.

To highlight this lack of interest in user safety and data privacy, we have the example of Facebook and Cambridge Analytica. In 2018, the Cambridge Analytica controversy came to light and sparked a debate about the difference between hacking and data brokering. Essentially, this was one of the first major news stories about information being unlawfully sold, not stolen. The data scraping[v] started in 2014 when 270,000 users participated in a personality quiz on Facebook, which was collected for a political consulting firm called Cambridge Analytica.[73] With a policy loophole, the company gained access to the complete profile data of not only the main user who took the test but also of every friend. In total, Cambridge

---

[v] *Data scrapping* is the process of converting what would otherwise be unusable/searchable material into usable/searchable material.

Analytica harvested more than fifty million profiles, with user data about their likes, friends, location, and more. Facebook claimed to have prohibited any of the collected data from being sold or transferred to any ad network, data broker, or other advertising or monetization-related service, but that didn't stop them. Cambridge Analytica used the illegal data to identify American personalities and influence voter behavior for the 2016 Trump campaign.[74] When the story first broke, Cambridge Analytica first denied that they had ever obtained or used any Facebook data.[75] The company then conceded that it was true and said that all of the information had been deleted. However, Facebook and dozens of news organizations, including the *New York Times*, were able to view the raw data sets, which still exist, and now, after widespread distribution, cannot ever be deleted fully.[76] Implications of these various behavior traits will be discussed later in regard to how by consumption patterns alone, you can be targeted to such a specific point of knowing when you are pregnant before you even know.

Advertisers and Marketers

Naturally, marketers want to get their hands on the most valuable consumer data in the world. Data has been referred to as the "new oil," but truthfully, it is more than that. It is an asset that increases in value the more it is used. Its importance lies in the fact that by its nature, it can be combined to provide insights for different stakeholders. Interestingly, data's value does not lie in its sale—its worth can be gauged by its potential to generate insights into market trends, consumer behavior, and shopping patterns. And most importantly, for our conversation here, social media sites have this data, and they are more than willing to grant companies access to it for a big payout. When advertisers pay to access your information, they can see the following:

- Which websites you have visited on any given day—and how long you stayed on the sites.

- Information you have saved or stored, like adding things to your shopping cart.

- All of your personal information and content sharing habits.

- Your interaction with other users on social media.

- GPS, saved photos, and voice data based on the app permissions.

With this information, advertisers engage in what is known as behavioral advertising, which means tailoring ads to an individual's personal interests.[77] Also known as *targeting*, behavioral advertising enables companies to create advertisements that they already know are going to pander to your interests. They then place the ads on social media sites and in the sidebars, hoping to turn you into a sale.

Children can be targets of this kind of advertising as well, especially political advertising. Therefore, if your teen approaches you about wanting to buy something they saw on social media, check it over first to see if it is a "brainwashing" attempt. Targeted advertising takes things a step farther, as companies and organizations can narrow the field to a particular demographic with personally identifiable information, like the kind of car you drive, your favorite sports team, or your political preference. Dynamic ads can even select a budget or luxury product when marketing to you, depending on your estimated income level.

The Facebook and Instagram mobile app brings these advertising tools to the masses with a more integrated marketing approach.

While users scroll through the app, advertisements are built right into the news feed for a more immersive experience instead of being sectioned off to the side of the screen in the ad section. As of 2018, approximately ninety-two percent of Facebook's entire advertising revenue comes from the mobile app.[78] Further, new video and Messenger ad strategies are becoming increasingly popular on the platform to supplement existing, proven advertising options.

Third-Party Apps

You know how you can click "Facebook login" with other apps today, like games and shopping apps? When you do that, you are granting the third-party app the ability to gather all of this social network information. After they access the information, they can use it to target you as well, or even sell it off to make their own profit.

When a third party is called into the question, the social media companies are no longer liable for what happens or what they do with your information. Therefore, here are a few things to consider:

- The third-party will not be included in the social media app's privacy policy. Consequently, they can do whatever they want.

- The third-party doesn't necessarily have to be secure.

- The third-party can use this information to market to you.

- The third-party may contain malware designed to attack your device.

While it may take a bit longer, when signing up on a new site, consider creating a new profile on the site rather than linking it to

Facebook and surrendering your data to them. Consider what sites your child is using that use the Facebook or Google login.

What About the Government?

This topic could be its own book, especially with my background at the CIA and FBI. There are a variety of countervailing forces that work against the government's use of and efforts to strengthen data privacy laws. Governments are lobbied by industries to keep limited restrictions on data in place, while advocacy groups demand protection of their data.[79, 80] At the same time, certain government agencies have incentives to reduce control over their ability to collect, store, and use these large data sets. Right now, government and law enforcement can monitor social networks for information needed to determine cases, dangerous scenarios, terrorism, etc. In the US, various government agencies monitor social networks for illegal activity, along with other digital information being created. While in China, the government does whatever it wants with any data at its disposal.

In 2013, Edward Snowden famously leaked documents from the National Security Agency (NSA) that revealed a secret surveillance program called PRISM. Ongoing investigations proved that the NSA had collected telephone records from millions of Verizon customers and was tracking customer activities through Microsoft, Google, and Apple.[81] The widespread access and surveillance of citizens affected nationwide platforms and corporations, ranging from emails and phone calls to video chat, audio, photographs, and documents.

The FBI deputy director explained how the program was used to profile, monitor, and track potential security threats. According to the FBI, the PRISM program was instrumental in successfully preventing dozens of planned terrorist attacks; however, numerous independent news agencies have discredited this statement. Despite Snowden's leak and public opinion against it, the program continued to function. According to reporting coming out of the *New York Times*, the program was only ordered to track forty targets in 2017, during which time the NSA collected 534 million records.[82] As of November 2019, the PRISM program was still active with government funding, but it was not currently being used to track targets.[83]

When iOS 8 rolled out in 2014, Apple increased encryption to unprecedented levels. At this time, even Apple could not access its own users' locked devices.[84] Public opinion across the nation was split when Apple refused to engineer a universal backdoor solution. Apple held firm and said that this digital protection and privacy was paramount to fundamental civil liberty.[85] Six weeks later, the FBI hired professional hackers from Israel to break into the phone at a cost of $900,000. The FBI's legal fight against Apple was immediately dropped as soon as they found a hacker who could work around the security. Some commentators saw this outcome as a win for privacy advocates and Apple, but in reality, it proved that with the right amount of money and hacker connections, the backdoor is more accessible than we'd like to think.

In February 2016, Apple executives were served with a forty-two-page writ from the government that ordered the company to comply with FBI demands. The FBI was trying to unlock a terrorist suspect's iPhone, but they could not crack the four-digit passcode. Apple engineers were already working with law enforcement to help them unlock the device, but the FBI demanded a backdoor system that could potentially unlock any iPhone instantly.

China?

Since I mentioned China, I need to provide some explanation for my specific grievances. Privacy is an especially important topic in China—the country with the largest population and the highest rates of reported privacy intrusions.

Digital tracking and censorship by the government have been highly controversial issues for nearly two decades. Likewise, data privacy is a controversial issue in China, with citizens and policymakers facing off on the topic. The Golden Shield Project is an example of an overarching government program that includes the Public Security and Supervision departments, which also maintain network control with a national firewall. The government's Great Firewall of China, as it is commonly known, actively blocks citizens from accessing foreign information sources and tools, including Google, Facebook, Twitter, Wikipedia, and more.

Recently, the Chinese government released a directory for managing personal data. Named the Information Security Technology—Personal Information Security Specification (PI-Specification), this rulebook covers data anonymization, access to personal information, data transfer, data breach notification, and the role and function of data controllers, among other topics. It was designed to facilitate China's existing laws on cybersecurity and consumer protection. In June 2019, China's apex administrative internet regulator, known as the Cyberspace Administration of China (CAC), released the Data Protection Regulatory Guideline. This move has changed the dynamics of regulations on privacy in China, as its stipulations clearly define personal data protection standards and serve as a reference point for future laws on the issue of privacy in China.

The government alone does not manage information censorship and online behavior monitoring. For non-Chinese companies to do business in the country, they must comply with local laws and regulations. In 2006, it was reported that at least three thousand companies had signed a public self-discipline pledge. This pledge acted as an agreement between the website or mobile app provider and the Chinese government to identify, prevent, and report any user information Chinese authorities would deem illicit or objectionable. Yahoo, Microsoft, and Google all signed the pledge in the early 2000s to provide partially censored access to Chinese citizens, which was highly controversial in the West.

China launched a three-part security plan that started in 2003 to build up a comprehensive citizen monitoring system. The first step was to record all citizens' IDs, photos, and information into a central database. Now, in 2019, the facial recognition system is estimated to be able to identify any person in mainland China within one second, and with 99.8 percent accuracy, according to Chinese state media.[86] A BBC reporter tested the system in cooperation with municipality police in 2017, when new AI assistive technology was unveiled. With the help of their extensive local CCTV monitoring system, police were able to locate and surround the BBC reporter in just seven minutes in this test by using only facial recognition data to track him.[87] In April 2019, facial recognition technology was used to track and apprehend a suspect who was hiding in a concert crowd of sixty thousand people.

In 2015, China officially started building a national video surveillance network. Just four years later, the Beijing Public Safety Bureau has reported that one hundred percent of Beijing is currently under surveillance and being monitored entirely by cameras. No other country in the world has such a comprehensive surveillance system, which has an estimated one hundred and seventy million CCTV cameras, as reported in October 2019. The massive infrastructure is still being built to canvass and monitor the entire nation under one network. Additionally, robot police have been installed in train stations to scan crowds and track fugitives with the facial recognition database. Law enforcement officers are now watching streets, transit stations, and crowded areas with AI-assisted facial recognition glasses, which were unveiled in early 2019.

Digital conversations are also being monitored closely. No major app in China offers encryption, except for Apple's iMessage, which some critics speculate is purposeful to allow government surveillance. WeChat, which hosts approximately one billion users every month, is required to store all conversation records for six months. All Chinese tech companies are required to report illegal activity and transfer data to the government upon request. Private WeChat and other group chat app transcripts have been used as evidence in criminal cases.

In the Xinjiang region, border agents are also installing malware on the phones of foreign travelers who enter the country at border crossings. This installation side-loads an app onto the phone, which has to be unlocked and handed over as part of a multi-step, intensive security checks, which can take up to half a day. Known as MobileHunter or CellHunter, the malware app downloads all of the device's text messages, calendar entries, emails, and phone logs. Reverse engineering has revealed that the system could also access usernames and data for many Android apps in addition to tracking what apps the user has downloaded. Additionally, the malware scans devices to look for more than seventy thousand logged suspicious files. The "suspicious material" ranges from ISIS and Al-Qaeda propaganda magazines to the writings of the Dalai Lama and historical content that is critical of China's involvement in Taiwan.

While traveling in the country, government agencies could utilize the scraped data to subsequently track the phone and movements with geotags and phone tower data.

The CellHunter malware was first discovered in July 2019 when travelers returned home and noticed the new, mysterious app. It's unclear how long this data hacking practice has been going on. Border officers were supposed to uninstall the app before returning the device to the traveler, but the app was "accidentally" handed back along with the phone.

And this is why I have to call China out in particular.

What About Employers?

One important distinction here is social vs. professional apps. We have discussed the mainly personal social media elements, but there is also a professional social media angle, such as LinkedIn. First of all, employers are allowed to view social profiles and make hiring decisions based on their findings. In fact, according to a CareerBuilder survey, seventy percent of employers use social media to screen candidates in the hiring process, while forty-three percent use social media to check in on current employees.[88, 89] Of course, discrimination is still not permitted, although more and more employers are using social media to make their final decisions today.

Once a person is hired, employers are allowed to monitor what is posted on social sites. Companies can limit what is posted to social profiles, as well as administer suspensions, etc. if the company is defamed on the social profiles. Additionally, there are many cases of employers being fired for the public remarks they thought were private.

In 2013, Justine Sacco was working as a senior director of corporate communications at IAC, which is a multinational media company. At the time, she only had one hundred and seventy Twitter followers, and her account was set to private, but that didn't stop an offensive tweet from going viral. Before getting on a plane, she tweeted, "Going to Africa. Hope I don't get AIDS. Just kidding. I'm white!"[90] After the eleven-hour flight, she turned on her phone again to discover that her message was the top trending tweet in the world. Tens of thousands of replies piled up, and she got an email from her company the same day to tell her that she was fired. She immediately deleted the tweet and her account, but she could not reverse the repercussions. This racist and insensitive scenario highlights how nothing is really private, and any message can make its way out of the sewer where it dwells.

Some states have fought back against employers making hiring/firing decisions on social media, passing various state laws asserting social media discrimination and silencing is illegal. But the argument in a company's defense is that social media posts have the potential to effect sales for the company, which is why it is something employers can take action against.

Of particular note in establishing some of the first data protection legislation was **the US Fair Credit Reporting Act (FCRA)**. This US law sets limits on what information employers can obtain from background checks. But the FCRA only applies to companies using third-party screening tools.

Social Media Privacy Policies

When you sign up on social media apps, you are free to read their privacy policy that is included in the fine print. However, it is important to remember that these apps can change these policies whenever they want. Just because what you said was protected four years ago, it does not mean that it still stands today. Additionally, their changes can also lead to changes in one's privacy settings. Always review that you have your settings set to the highest. Also, take the time to read over the policies every few months for your teen's sake. You will be surprised how much data is surrendered in these agreements.

Final Online Privacy Tips

What can you tell your child that will help them not only retain their personal information more effectively but also keep their accounts protected from cyber attackers?

- *Use unique passwords.* Do not recycle the same passwords over and over again. If a hacker can determine your password on one profile, they will be able to access all of your profiles. When this happens, they can steal your information and identity or post defamatory content that is racist or homophobic—getting your teen in trouble when they didn't really do it.

- *Skew your security questions.* If a question asks you for your mother's first name, throw the person off and put down a totally bogus name. Just be sure to copy it all down in a secure file, so you don't end up locked out of your account.

- *Use a social-media-only email address.* The less connection between your social media accounts and personal life, the better. Consider an email address that is just made for social sites.

- *Always review privacy policies.* This might sound boring, but it's an essential step in staying abreast of online safety for your teen.

- *Do not use social media logins with third-party apps.* Make a unique profile so that there is no connection between the two.

- *Don't divulge unnecessary information.* No one needs to know your employer. Keep as much information off of your profiles as possible. This is appropriate for professional apps, but still be careful.

- *Reject friend requests from strangers.* Teach your kids to decline any rogue friend requests that are not from people they already know. There is no need to give these random strangers access to such pertinent information.

- *Log off from social media sites when you are done using them.* Otherwise, they can remain "on" in the background of your phone, possibly aggregating more information. There have been suggestions that these apps use your camera and microphone to watch you and listen to you.

Chapter 6

How Parents Can Be Proactive

Privacy is dead, and social media holds the smoking gun.
—Pete Cashmore

The chapter we have all been waiting for! As a parent, you want to know how you can be proactive. You do not just want to sit by while your child disappears down the social media rabbit hole. You want them back, present, and happy at the dinner table, with their phone in their pocket and their attitude in a positive place.

We want that for you too. Social media is not going anywhere, and it sure is not an easy problem to deal with. But there is always room for parents to be proactive. Your kids will take notice, and they will know that they have a friend in you if something goes wrong online.

Here is how you can be proactive.

Start the Social Media Discussion Early

Even if social media is not part of your household, it is undoubtedly part of the households that your child will be visiting when they have sleepovers or visit friends. Since the average kid is getting on social media between the ages of ten and twelve, your kid will be introduced to this world whether you like it or not.[91]

Therefore, you must start the conversation about social media with your child at a young age. Even if kids are not on social media, many kids are still using a variety of websites and gaming platforms that expose them to the digital world. In this world, these websites and apps and your child's friends shape their digital education. It is important that parents take an active role in encouraging conversations about the role of social media in one's life.

Although this may seem like an awkward conversation you do not want to have, it's one that needs to happen, nonetheless. Some of the obvious things you should cover in these conversations (that should occur around the age of nine or ten) are as follows:

- **Privacy settings:** Build a relationship with your child in which you don't preach to them about privacy online. Offer up your help to ensure their profiles are protected, with no trace of judgment in your voice.

- **Posting rules:** Go over what kind of content should be shared and shouldn't be shared online. Make a game out of it!

- **Warn them of dangers:** No one wants to scare a ten-year-old, but with social media today, these conversations need to be had. Talk to them about predators and sexual activity on social media, so they know you are aware of what is going on.

- **Your support:** Let them know that above all else, you are there for them and can help. With social anxiety over social media and a rise in cyberbullying, kids need to know they have a support network. Reach out to a school counselor or other trusted adult to build a positive network for them.

These are just a few ideas for what to include in that initial conversation, which should be a regular conversation in your home. Stay aware, stay engaged, and stay informed. Knowing these issues will help prepare your child for the digital problems of today and the future.

Make a Plan

It is best to come from a place of curiosity and open-ended questions when working with your children to help them identify why they want to join Instagram, etc. Ask them about what they believe Instagram will do for them, what a positive experience on Instagram will look like, and what they've heard from their friends about Instagram.

Inquisitive questions like those that start with "how" show them that they are equals who are going to try to teach you something. I always used curiosity-based questions to drive my work.

Asking these questions allows your child to think about how they would define their perception of social media. When they answer the questions, you will be able to see where they are coming from on it and work with them to make a plan.

As part of your plan, go over the three S's:

- **Healthy socialization:** Talk about how much socialization is healthy and how much is too much.

- **Self-regulation:** Social media is a big place, which means we all need to take responsibility for ourselves.

- **Safety:** Go over tips for how your teen can be safe when using social media. This goes back to our points of not

accepting friend requests from people they do not know,
having high-security settings, limiting what they post, and
not disclosing personally identifiable information.

Privacy, Privacy, and More Privacy

Ensure every single element of your child's social media is private,
verifying that they limit what data they post and preventing these
sites from accessing additional data. As noted, high privacy settings
will limit their exposure to unwanted viewers. Advise them on
limiting what they publish, since nothing online is ever truly private.
Finally, and most importantly, limit the accesses you grant any
application, social media, or otherwise. There is no reason
Facebook or any of these other apps need to access your GPS data.
For example, several games for kids access their GPS data on the
phone even though it is really just a Candy Crush knockoff. There
are countless examples of games and applications that access more
than they need for the app to operate. Although your information
can still be sold to companies, at least take the time to ensure your
profiles and your child's profiles cannot be searched or located by
other users.

When you approach your child with a sense of openness and
support, they will be much more likely to allow you to help them
ensure everything is private. Be with them when they make the
profiles, so they feel like you are on their side.

Go Over Social Media Etiquette

Explain to your child that defamatory comments, swearing, and
anything else they post on social media can be seen by everyone.
Even if it is in a private chat, people are going to take screenshots
and share the text with as many people as they want. Therefore,
anything said on social media needs to be considered public, even if

the account is private. I may seem like a broken record, but I cannot overstate that enough. Additionally, the most important social media tool for your children is to learn how to save, block, and report any inappropriate material or cyberbullying/cyberhate. Every social media platform may be slightly unique in where the "report button" is, but sit down with them and show them how to block and report issues.

Other social media etiquette tips include:

- Going over how it is not appropriate to post ten plus times per day. No one wants their newsfeed flooded. This will also support a healthy balance between social media and work life. It is okay if they do not respond to every message or post within seconds.

- Being nice to people on social media. As we mentioned many times before, nothing is private, and any nasty messages can easily be spread across the whole internet.

- What notifications mean and why turning them off is a great way to ensure some balance.

Setting Time Limits

It is perfectly acceptable to set social media time limits, so your child does not develop too much of an addiction. At most, permit them to get on their phones from the time they get home from school until dinner, and then for one hour after dinner (only if their homework is already done). Lead by example. Consider putting away your work phone when you are at the dinner table to show that there is a place and time for certain interactions.

After that, it is time to put the phone down and be in the moment. Make sure that you still give the child time to be on social media, if you are going to take it away from them for certain hours of the day. Making this a habit will make them less angry and more likely to understand that taking a break from their phone is good for their physical and mental health.

Talk About Accountability

Accountability is something wholly lacking from our society today, causing problems in a variety of ways. If your child becomes a victim of cyberbullying, they are accountable to do something about it. They can report comments and accounts, as well as flag users to Instagram. They can tell you and their friends so that other people are aware of the problem.

Without this kind of accountability, it will be hard for you to come to their aid. Explain to them that you won't necessarily know if cyberbullying is occurring, which is why it's up to them to make you aware so you can help.

Be a Good Example

Remember, you are on social media too. If you are friends with your teen, they can see what YOU post. Are you proud of your social media profile? Do you write mean things under political posts? Do you post inappropriate content? Are you addicted to your phone?

Your child is watching your every move. You need to make sure your social media presence is squeaky clean, so they can see that you mean what you say. Without even realizing it, they are going to follow your lead.

That means that, yes, it's time for you to follow all of the rules and tips we've just set out in this book. You are not immune to the effects of social media either. Social media affects us all, and it's going to continue to do so for a very, very long time.

> *We don't have a choice on whether we do social media, the question is how well we do it.*[92]
> **—Erik Qualman**

As the quote above states, we don't have a choice when it comes to social media. It has infiltrated every part of our lives, and frankly, we've let it. We cannot make it through half a day without picking up our phones and opening some kind of social media app. At this point, you know why. Don't fight it. It's a waste of energy.

Instead, welcome it in and make your home one of social media tolerance and understanding. Maybe you do a weekly family social media meeting where you learn about one new thing on social apps. Whatever you do, make it a non-"taboo" topic so your teen feels like they can come to you with any social media concerns or questions.

With this kind of trusting relationship, you can ensure your teen never ends up on the wrong side of cyberbullying, depressed, alone, and anxious.

The digital world is a massive, astonishing, and also highly dangerous place. Conversations need to take place between you, your children, and even your spouse. Liken social media to the nightly news—it's part of our habitual lives.

Conclusion

This social media awareness guide can be broken down into two key topics. The first is understanding social media, what sites are out there, and the risks to your child. The second is how social media, and many sites in general, are harvesting your child's personal identity and what that means for their future.

The first is a constantly shifting target as different social media platforms skyrocket into greatness and then fade into the background as new, hotter platforms make their ascension. This is the case with the Facebook platform. However, the Facebook company has built a war chest allowing it to catch any shooting stars in the social media world. Therefore, by being educated on the current applications out there and how children use them, you can better understand how your children are likely to engage with each other now and into the future. Additionally, understanding the psychological ramifications of social media in children's health will also help you see the challenges in navigating this tool that is not going away.

The second half of the book was the privacy and personal data issue. One of technology's gifts to humanity is the internet, and throughout this book, we have been talking about its offspring, social media. The internet has revolutionized how we live and has increased our potential to achieve even greater things. Yet the internet has destroyed quite a few people and hurt lots more. The internet is built on information exchange, and most of our everyday tasks are linked to the web in one way or another. Social media companies are at the center of much of this data creation and marketing. We find it easy to give away valuable information (data) about ourselves for a "free" email account or "free" social media access.

Increased outcry over the damages generated by data privacy issues sparked debates and the furor that led to new legal restrictions. However, these appear to do little in stemming the tide of the data breach and other more damaging situations.

Data is now seen as a near-indispensable resource that is being harvested at all costs. Its current status has led to the growth of the billion-dollar data brokerage industry. This industry engages in the gathering, storing, and selling of personal data that is both valuable to the legal and illegal aspects of the cyber world. The sustained growth of the data brokerage industry portends the death of data privacy.

Lots of personal data is collected and gathered, mostly without consent. Despite the presence of online privacy policies, it would appear that the practice of scraping, storing, and selling user data will not stop anytime soon, especially as private businesses will always put profit before their customers—anything for a buck. Security laws and protection offer little in terms of a haven from data privacy issues. The responsibility rests with the user, who must do all in their power to keep their personal data safe. Staying secure is a difficult but possible task that is well worth the time and effort. And with all of this, there is an extensive list of applications, social media and otherwise, sitting on your child's phone that is being sent to a server bank somewhere to later be used for targeting your child with advertising and political marketing.

We do not need to run from any of these topics. We need to look at the good and bad elements and isolate the negative ones. The first step starts at home with you and your kids as you tell them about privacy settings and limiting what data is published online. The second step is accomplished by talking to your schools to make sure they are creating an environment where kids know how to stay safe in a digital world and report any predators, suicidal ideations, and cyberbullying/cyberhate. Most of the schools I have talked to are not equipped to deal with any or most of these issues. And finally, take steps to lobby your legislators to enact legislation to protect children's rights online and ensure data privacy. Policymakers need to be held accountable when they fail to create privacy laws that promotes a healthy future for our children.

Therefore, if this book means anything, take this as a call to action to change how we see and interact with the internet for the betterment of future generations.

Security Squad

We are the only interactive platform designed specifically to help kids and teens become more aware of how they can safely interact with the digital world while preparing for the future. This interactive platform is in the form of educational comic books, educational videogames, and lesson plans for teachers and homeschoolers. As we work to build this comprehensive service and bring it to a school near you, we also welcome your help in challenging what material is being taught to your kids. Is your school teaching your kids about cybersecurity, cyberbullying, social media interactions, online strangers, and coding? If not, then we need to ask why, because these skills are essential in our digital life.

Furthermore, beyond identifying threats, Security Squad is also working to help kids develop the skills they need to find jobs in cybersecurity, business intelligence, and other tech-related fields that are in desperate need of young talent today.

We're embracing this new digitally social age with openness so we can find solutions to the problems it creates. We urge you to do the same.

What Did You Think of A Parent's Guide to Teen Social Media:

What Your Kids Aren't Telling You?

First of all, thank you for purchasing this book, *A Parent's Guide to Teen Social Media: What Your Kids Aren't Telling You*. I know you could have picked any number of books to read, but you picked this book, and for that I am extremely grateful.

I hope that it added value and quality to your everyday life. If so, it would be really nice if you could share this book with your friends and family by posting about it on Facebook and Twitter.

If you enjoyed this book and found some benefit, I would like to hear from you. Please post a review on Amazon. Your feedback and support will help me to improve my future projects and books.

You can now follow this link to https://www.amazon.com/dp/B087JVDJMJ/ref=cm_sw_em_r_mt_dp_U_OzYOEbPET7JEJ.

[1] "A Quote by Germany Kent." *Goodreads*, Goodreads, www.goodreads.com/quotes/3204865-you-are-responsible-for-everything-you-post-and-everything-you.

[2] Tatera, Kelly. "Is It Possible to Imagine Infinity in Our Minds?" *The Science Explorer*, 6 Nov. 2015, thescienceexplorer.com/brain-and-body/it-possible-imagine-infinity-our-minds.

[3] Phillips, Sarah. "A Brief History of Facebook." *The Guardian*, Guardian News and Media, 25 July 2007, www.theguardian.com/technology/2007/jul/25/media.newmedia.

[4] Kallas, Priit. "Top 15 Most Popular Social Networking Sites and Apps [2020] @DreamGrow." *DreamGrow*, 2 Sept. 2019, www.dreamgrow.com/top-15-most-popular-social-networking-sites/.

[5] Whiting, Kate. "Coronavirus Isn't an Outlier, It's Part of Our Interconnected Viral Age." *World Economic Forum*, 4 Mar. 2020, www.weforum.org/agenda/2020/03/coronavirus-global-epidemics-health-pandemic-covid-19/.

[6] Swartz, Jon, and Jessica Guynn. "Facebook's Mark Zuckerberg Steps into Political Fray." *USA Today*, 13 Apr. 2016, eu.usatoday.com/story/tech/2016/04/12/zuckerbergs-10-year-plan-expand-facebook-empire/82936814/.

[7] Phillips, Sarah. "A Brief History of Facebook." *The Guardian*, Guardian News and Media, 25 July 2007, www.theguardian.com/technology/2007/jul/25/media.newmedia.

[8] "Facebook's Data-Sharing Deals Exposed." *BBC News*, BBC, 19 Dec. 2018, www.bbc.com/news/technology 46618582.

[9] Lam, Kristin. "Mark Zuckerberg: Facebook Has Stopped Russia and Iran

Campaigns to Meddle in 2020 Election." *USA Today*, Gannett Satellite Information Network, 15 Dec. 2019, eu.usatoday.com/story/news/nation/2019/10/21/facebook-election-interference-russia-iran-campaigns-2020-mark-zuckerberg/4059431002/.

[10] Liao, Shannon. "After the Porn Ban, Tumblr Users Have Ditched the Platform as Promised." *The Verge*, 14 Mar. 2019, www.theverge.com/2019/3/14/18266013/tumblr-porn-ban-lost-users-down-traffic.

[11] Cook, Gareth. "Why We Are Wired to Connect." *Scientific American*, Scientific American, 22 Oct. 2013, www.scientificamerican.com/article/why-we-are-wired-to-connect/.

[12] Formica, Michael J. "Why We Care About What Other People Think of Us." *Psychology Today*, 31 Dec. 2014, www.psychologytoday.com/us/blog/enlightened-living/201412/why-we-care-about-what-other-people-think-us.

[13] Schomer, Audrey. "Influencer Marketing: State of the Social Media Influencer Market in 2020." *Business Insider*, 17 Dec. 2019, www.businessinsider.com/influencer-marketing-report?IR=T.

[14] Sterling, Greg. "Nearly 80 Percent of Social Media Time Now Spent on Mobile Devices." *Marketing Land*, 4 Apr. 2016, marketingland.com/facebook-usage-accounts-1-5-minutes-spent-mobile-171561.

[15] Swanson, Emily. "Instagram and Snapchat Are Most Popular Social Networks for Teens; Black Teens Are Most Active on Social Media, Messaging Apps." Instagram and Snapchat Are Most Popular Social Networks for Teens; Black Teens Are Most Active on Social Media, Messaging Apps | APNORC.org, apnorc.org/projects/pages/html reports/instagram-and-snapchat-are-most-popular-social-networks-for-teens.aspx.

[16] "A Quote from The Social Media Mind." *Goodreads*, Goodreads, www.goodreads.com/quotes/791924-social-media-is-addictive-precisely-

because-it-gives-us-something.

[17] Brigham, Katie. "Facebook, Snapchat and TikTok Have a Massive Underage User Problem—Here's Why It Matters." *CNBC*, 22 Dec. 2018, www.cnbc.com/2018/12/21/what-age-is-appropriate-to-sign-up-for-social-media.html.

[18] Lenhart, Amanda, and Mary Madden. "Friendship, Strangers and Safety in Online Social Networks." *Pew Research Center: Internet, Science & Tech*, Pew Research Center, 18 Apr. 2007, www.pewresearch.org/internet/2007/04/18/friendship-strangers-and-safety-in-online-social-networks/.

[19] Grigonis, Hillary K. "1 In 5 Teenagers Are Bullied Online, New Cyberbullying Statistics Suggest." *Digital Trends*, 20 July 2017, www.digitaltrends.com/social-media/cyberbullying-statistics-2017-ditch-the-label/.

[20] Simmons, Rachel. "How Social Media Is a Toxic Mirror." *Time*, 19 Aug. 2016, time.com/4459153/social-media-body-image/.

[21] Holland, Grace, and Marika Tiggemann. "A Systematic Review of the Impact of the Use of Social Networking Sites on Body Image and Disordered Eating Outcomes." *Research Gate*, June 2016, https://www.citationmachine.net/bibliographies/585390900?new=true.

[22] Stefanone, Machael A., et al. "Contingencies of Self-Worthand Social-Networking-Site Behavior." *University of Buffalo*, vol. 14, no. 1-2, 2011, doi:10.1089/cyber.2010.004.

[23] "37 TikTok Statistics That Will Blow Your Mind [INFOGRAPHIC]." *Influencer Marketing Hub*, 19 Mar. 2020, influencermarketinghub.com/tiktok-statistics/.

[24] Peterson, Taylor. "TikTok vs. Snapchat: A Guide for Marketers." *Marketing Land*, 4 Mar. 2020, marketingland.com/tiktok-vs-snapchat-a-guide-for-marketers-276820.

25 "TikTok by the Numbers: Stats, Demographics & Fun Facts." *Omnicore*, 12 Feb. 2020, www.omnicoreagency.com/tiktok-statistics/.

26 Tran, Tony. "Instagram Demographics That Matter to Social Media Marketers in 2020." *Hootsuite Social Media Management*, 4 Feb. 2020, blog.hootsuite.com/instagram-demographics/.

27 "Instagram Demographics: 13 Impressive Statistics About Instagram Users." Mediakix, 19 Oct. 2018, mediakix.com/blog/13-impressive-instagram-demographics-user-statistics-to-see/.

28 Tran, Tony. "Instagram Demographics That Matter to Social Media Marketers in 2020." *Hootsuite Social Media Management*, 4 Feb. 2020, blog.hootsuite.com/instagram-demographics/.

29 Smith, Kit. "57 Fascinating and Incredible YouTube Statistics." *Brandwatch*, 21 Feb. 2020, www.brandwatch.com/blog/youtube-stats/.

30 "37 Mind Blowing YouTube Facts, Figures and Statistics—2020." *Merch Dope*, 26 Feb. 2020, merchdope.com/youtube-stats/.

31 Popper, Ben. "YouTube's Biggest Star Is a 5-Year-Old That Makes Millions Opening Toys." *The Verge*, 22 Dec. 2016, www.theverge.com/2016/12/22/14031288/ryan-toys-review-biggest-youngest-youtube-star-millions.

32 Binder, Matt. "YouTube Removes More than 100,000 Videos for Violating Its Hate Speech Policy." *Mashable*, 3 Sept. 2019, mashable.com/article/youtube-hate-speech-policy-removals/.

33 Alexander, Julia. "More than 17,000 YouTube Channels Removed since New Hateful Content Policy Implemented." *The Verge*, 3 Sept. 2019, www.theverge.com/2019/9/3/20845071/youtube-hateful-content-policies-channels-comments-videos-susan-wojcicki.

34 "Snapchat Demographics & Statistics That May Surprise You [Infographic]."

Mediakix, 21 Mar. 2019, mediakix.com/blog/snapchat-demographics-infographic-statistics/.

35 CBS News. "Kik Messenger App Scrutinized Following 13-Year-Old's Death." *CBS News*, 3 Feb. 2016, www.cbsnews.com/news/kik-messenger-app-scrutinized-following-13-year-olds-death/.

36 Statt, Nick. "WhatsApp Co-Founder Jan Koum Is Leaving Facebook after Clashing over Data Privacy." *The Verge*, 30 Apr. 2018, www.theverge.com/2018/4/30/17304792/whatsapp-jan-koum-facebook-data-privacy-encryption.

37 Anderson, Monica. "Parents, Teens and Digital Monitoring." *Pew Research Center: Internet, Science & Tech*, Pew Research Center, 7 Jan. 2016, www.pewresearch.org/internet/2016/01/07/parents-teens-and-digital-monitoring/.

38 Anderson, Monica. "Parents, Teens and Digital Monitoring." *Pew Research Center: Internet, Science & Tech*, Pew Research Center, 7 Jan. 2016, www.pewresearch.org/internet/2016/01/07/parents-teens-and-digital-monitoring/.

39 Anderson, Monica. "Parents, Teens and Digital Monitoring." *Pew Research Center: Internet, Science & Tech*, Pew Research Center, 7 Jan. 2016, www.pewresearch.org/internet/2016/01/07/parents-teens-and-digital-monitoring/.

40 Anderson, Monica. "Parents, Teens and Digital Monitoring." *Pew Research Center: Internet, Science & Tech*, Pew Research Center, 7 Jan. 2016, www.pewresearch.org/internet/2016/01/07/parents-teens-and-digital-monitoring/.

41 Anderson, Monica. "Parents, Teens and Digital Monitoring." *Pew Research Center: Internet, Science & Tech*, Pew Research Center, 7 Jan. 2016, www.pewresearch.org/internet/2016/01/07/parents-teens-and-digital-monitoring/.

[42] Anderson, Monica. "Parents, Teens and Digital Monitoring." *Pew Research Center: Internet, Science & Tech*, Pew Research Center, 7 Jan. 2016, www.pewresearch.org/internet/2016/01/07/parents-teens-and-digital-monitoring/.

[43] Anderson, Monica. "1. How Parents Monitor Their Teen's Digital Behavior." *Pew Research Center: Internet, Science & Tech*, Pew Research Center, 7 Jan. 2016, www.pewresearch.org/internet/2016/01/07/how-parents-monitor-their-teens-digital-behavior/.

[44] "A Quote by Steven Furtick." *Goodreads*, Goodreads, www.goodreads.com/quotes/1128481-the-reason-we-struggle-with-insecurity-is-because-we-compare.

[45] Lally, Phillippa, et al. "How Are Habits Formed: Modelling Habit Formation in the Real World." *Wiley Online Library*, John Wiley & Sons, Ltd, 16 July 2009, onlinelibrary.wiley.com/doi/abs/10.1002/ejsp.674.

[46] Rogers, Kristen. "US Teens Use Screens More than Seven Hours a Day on Average." *CNN*, Cable News Network, 29 Oct. 2019, edition.cnn.com/2019/10/29/health/common-sense-kids-media-use-report-wellness/index.html.

[47] Walton, Alice G. "6 Ways Social Media Affects Our Mental Health." *Forbes*, Forbes Magazine, 30 June 2017, www.forbes.com/sites/alicegwalton/2017/06/30/a-run-down-of-social-medias-effects-on-our-mental-health/.

[48] Chan, Terri H. "Facebook and Its Effects on Users' Empathic Social Skills and Life Satisfaction: A Double-Edged Sword Effect." *Research Gate*, Mar. 2014, www.researchgate.net/publication/260643177_Facebook_and_its_Effects_on_Users'_Empathic_Social_Skills_and_Life_Satisfaction_A_Double-Edged_Sword_Effect.

[49] Chan, Terri H. "Facebook and Its Effects on Users' Empathic Social Skills and

Life Satisfaction: A Double-Edged Sword Effect." *Research Gate*, Mar. 2014, www.researchgate.net/publication/260643177_Facebook_and_its_Effects_on_Users'_Empathic_Social_Skills_and_Life_Satisfaction_A_Double-Edged_Sword_Effect.

[50] Ro, Christine. "Dunbar's Number: Why We Can Only Maintain 150 Relationships." *BBC* , 9 Oct. 2019, www.bbc.com/future/article/20191001-dunbars-number-why-we-can-only-maintain-150-relationships.

[51] Barr, Sabrina. "Six Ways Social Media Negatively Affects Your Mental Health without You Even Knowing." *The Independent*, Independent Digital News and Media, 10 Oct. 2019, www.independent.co.uk/life-style/health-and-families/social-media-mental-health-negative-effects-depression-anxiety-addiction-memory-a8307196.html.

[52] Barr, Sabrina. "Six Ways Social Media Negatively Affects Your Mental Health without You Even Knowing." *The Independent*, Independent Digital News and Media, 10 Oct. 2019, www.independent.co.uk/life-style/health-and-families/social-media-mental-health-negative-effects-depression-anxiety-addiction-memory-a8307196.html.

[53] "More than 1 in 20 US Children and Teens Have Anxiety or Depression." *ScienceDaily*, ScienceDaily, 24 Apr. 2018, www.sciencedaily.com/releases/2018/04/180424184119.htm.

[54] Miller, Caroline. "Does Social Media Cause Depression?" *Child Mind Institute*, childmind.org/article/is-social-media-use-causing-depression/.

[55] McAteer, Oliver. "Gen Z Is Quitting Social Media in Droves Because It Makes Them Unhappy, Study Finds." *PR Week*, PR Week Global, 9 Mar. 2018, www.prweek.com/article/1459149/gen-z-quitting-social-media-droves-makes-unhappy-study-finds.

[56] McAteer, Oliver. "Gen Z Is Quitting Social Media in Droves Because It Makes Them Unhappy, Study Finds." *PR Week*, PR Week Global, 9 Mar. 2018, www.prweek.com/article/1459149/gen-z-quitting-social-media-droves-makes-

unhappy-study-finds.

57 Heid, Markham. "Depression and Suicide Rates Are Rising Sharply in Young Americans, New Report Says." *Time*, 14 Mar. 2019, time.com/5550803/depression-suicide-rates-youth/.

58 "Adolescence." Psychology Today, www.psychologytoday.com/intl/basics/adolescence.

59 Daniels, Natasha. "Beyond Stranger Danger: Tips That Can Save Your Kid's Life." *AT: Parenting Survival for All Ages*, www.anxioustoddlers.com/stranger-danger/#.XefR_pNKjOQ.

60 Kempf, Victoria. "Stats About Online Predators and Precautions Parents Should Take." *Patch*, 12 Mar. 2012, patch.com/massachusetts/sudbury/bp--stats-about-online-predators-and-precautions-parec47b01a336.

61 Jaschik, Scott. "Decline Found in Colleges That Check Applicants' Social Media." *Inside Higher ED*, 3 Dec. 2018, www.insidehighered.com/admissions/article/2018/12/03/survey-finds-decline-share-colleges-check-applicants-social-media.

62 Driver, Saige. "Social Media Screenings Increase for Job Seekers." *Business News Daily*, 7 Oct. 2018, www.businessnewsdaily.com/2377-social-media-hiring.html.

63 Hanke, Stacey. "How Social Media Affects Our Ability to Communicate." *Thrive Global*, 13 Sept. 2018, thriveglobal.com/stories/how-social-media-affects-our-ability-to-communicate/.

64 "Gen Z and Millennials Now More Likely to Communicate with Each Other Digitally than in Person - Oct 17, 2017." *LivePerson*. PRNewswire, 17 Oct. 2017, pr.liveperson.com/index.php?s=43&item=504.

65 Wortham, Jenna. "A Pair of Social Media Predicaments." The New York Times, The New York Times, 23 Nov. 2009,

gadgetwise.blogs.nytimes.com/2009/11/23/a-pair-of-social-media-predicaments/.

[66] Curtin, Melanie. "Bill Gates Says This Is the 'Safest' Age to Give a Child a Smartphone." *Inc.com*, 10 May 2017, www.inc.com/melanie-curtin/bill-gates-says-this-is-the-safest-age-to-give-a-child-a-smartphone.html.

[67] "Data Protection Act 2018." *UK Public General Acts*, 23 May 2018, www.legislation.gov.uk/ukpga/2018/12/enacted.

[68] Hill, Kashmir. "How Target Figured Out A Teen Girl Was Pregnant Before Her Father Did." *Forbes*, Forbes Magazine, 16 Feb. 2012, www.forbes.com/sites/kashmirhill/2012/02/16/how-target-figured-out-a-teen-girl-was-pregnant-before-her-father-did/.

[69] "FTC Imposes $5 Billion Penalty and Sweeping New Privacy Restrictions on Facebook." *Federal Trade Commission*, 24 July 2019, www.ftc.gov/news-events/press-releases/2019/07/ftc-imposes-5-billion-penalty-sweeping-new-privacy-restrictions.

[70] Wong, Julia Carrie. "Facebook Revenues Soar despite $5.1bn in Fines and New Antitrust Investigation." *The Guardian*, Guardian News and Media, 24 July 2019, www.theguardian.com/technology/2019/jul/24/facebook-revenue-fines-second-quarter.

[71] Satariano, Adam. "Google Is Fined $57 Million Under Europe's Data Privacy Law." *The New York Times*, 21 Jan. 2019, www.nytimes.com/2019/01/21/technology/google-europe-gdpr-fine.html.

[72] Sirota, Dimitri. "California's New Data Privacy Law Brings U.S. Closer to GDPR." *TechCrunch*, 14 Nov. 2019, techcrunch.com/2019/11/14/californias-new-data-privacy-law-brings-u-s-closer-to-gdpr/.

[73] Lapowsky, Issie. "Facebook Exposed 87 Million Users to Cambridge Analytica." *Wired*, 4 Apr. 2018, www.wired.com/story/facebook-exposed-87-million-users-to-cambridge-analytica/.

74 Lapowsky, Issie. "Facebook Exposed 87 Million Users to Cambridge Analytica." *Wired*, 4 Apr. 2018, www.wired.com/story/facebook-exposed-87-million-users-to-cambridge-analytica/.

75 Ma, Alexandra, and Ben Gilbert. "Facebook Understood How Dangerous the Trump-Linked Data Firm Cambridge Analytica Could Be Much Earlier than It Previously Said. Here's Everything That's Happened up until Now." Business Insider, 23 Aug. 2019, www.businessinsider.com/cambridge-analytica-a-guide-to-the-trump-linked-data-firm-that-harvested-50-million-facebook-profiles-2018-3?IR=T#does-this-change-facebook-and-cambridge-analyticas-previous-testimonies-6.

76 Granville, Kevin. "Facebook and Cambridge Analytica: What You Need to Know as Fallout Widens." *The New York Times*, 19 Mar. 2018, www.nytimes.com/2018/03/19/technology/facebook-cambridge-analytica-explained.html.

77 "Social Networking Privacy: How to Be Safe, Secure and Social." Privacy Rights Clearinghouse, 25 Mar. 2019, privacyrights.org/consumer-guides/social-networking-privacy-how-be-safe-secure-and-social.

78 Clement, J. "Facebook: Mobile Ad Revenue Share 2018." *Statista*, 3 Feb. 2020, www.statista.com/statistics/462370/share-of-mobile-facebook-ad-revenue/.

79 Lapowsky, Issie. "Tech Lobbyists Push to Defang California's Landmark Privacy Law." *Wired*, 29 Apr. 2019, www.wired.com/story/california-privacy-law-tech-lobby-bills-weaken/.

80 Reed Albergotti, Tony Romm. "Apple Preaches Privacy. Lawmakers Want the Talk to Turn to Action." *The Washington Post*, WP Company, 15 July 2019, www.washingtonpost.com/technology/2019/07/15/apple-preaches-privacy-lawmakers-want-talk-turn-action/.

81 Greenwald, Glenn, and Ewen MacAskill. "NSA Prism Program Taps in to User Data of Apple, Google and Others." *The Guardian*, Guardian News and Media, 7

June 2013, www.theguardian.com/world/2013/jun/06/us-tech-giants-nsa-data.

[82] Savage, Charlie. "Disputed N.S.A. Phone Program Is Shut Down, Aide Says." *The New York Times*, 4 Mar. 2019, www.nytimes.com/2019/03/04/us/politics/nsa-phone-records-program-shut-down.html.

[83] Savage, Charlie. "Disputed N.S.A. Phone Program Is Shut Down, Aide Says." *The New York Times*, 4 Mar. 2019, www.nytimes.com/2019/03/04/us/politics/nsa-phone-records-program-shut-down.html.

[84] Farivar, Cyrus. "Apple Expands Data Encryption under IOS 8, Making Handover to Cops Moot." *Ars Technica*, 18 Sept. 2014, arstechnica.com/gadgets/2014/09/apple-expands-data-encryption-under-ios-8-making-handover-to-cops-moot/.

[85] Domonoske, Camila, and Alina Selyukh. "Why Apple Says It Won't Help Unlock That IPhone, In 5 Key Quotes." *NPR*, 25 Feb. 2016, www.npr.org/sections/thetwo-way/2016/02/25/468158520/why-apple-says-it-wont-help-unlock-that-iphone-in-5-key-quotes.

[86] Yusha, Zhao. "'Sky Net' Tech Fast Enough to Scan Chinese Population in One Second: Report." Global Times, 25 Mar. 2018, www.globaltimes.cn/content/1095176.shtml.

[87] Liu, Joyce. "In Your Face: China's All-Seeing State." *BBC News*, 10 Dec. 2017, www.bbc.com/news/av/world-asia-china-42248056/in-your-face-china-s-all-seeing-state.

[88] Driver, Saige. "Social Media Screenings Increase for Job Seekers." *Business News Daily*, 7 Oct. 2018, www.businessnewsdaily.com/2377-social-media-hiring.html.

[89] "More Than Half of Employers Have Found Content on Social Media That Caused Them NOT to Hire a Candidate, According to Recent CareerBuilder Survey." *PR Newswire*, 9 Aug. 2018, www.prnewswire.com/news-releases/more-than-half-of-employers-have-found-content-on-social-media-that-caused-them-

not-to-hire-a-candidate-according-to-recent-careerbuilder-survey-300694437.html.

[90] Ronson, Jon. "How One Stupid Tweet Blew Up Justine Sacco's Life." *The New York Times*, 12 Feb. 2015, www.nytimes.com/2015/02/15/magazine/how-one-stupid-tweet-ruined-justine-saccos-life.html.

[91] Tode, Chantal. "50pc Of Kids Have Social Media Accounts by Age 12: Report." *Mobile Marketer*, www.mobilemarketer.com/ex/mobilemarketer/cms/news/research/22866.html.

[92] Qualman, Erik. "A Quote by Erik Qualman." *Goodreads*, Goodreads, www.goodreads.com/quotes/729544-we-don-t-have-a-choice-on-whether-we-do-social.